The Kingdom

Experience Heaven on Earth Part II

Dr. Kelafo Collie, M.D.
Shallaywa Collie, MBA

Copyright ©2020 Dr. Kelafo Z. Collie, M.D.,

Shallaywa Collie, MBA

The Kingdom

Experience Heaven on Earth Part II

ISBN 978-1-7355413-5-8

All rights reserved. No part of this book may be reproduced or transmitted in any form or by any means without written permission.

www.kelafozcollie.com

www.shallaywa.com

Published by:

Majestic Priesthood Publication,

Freeport, Grand Bahama, Bahamas.

Email: mpppublications@gmail.com

1-242-727-2137

Printed in the United States of America

CONTENTS

INTRODUCTION 5

CHAPTER 1. THE MYSTERIES AND THE TRUTH OF THE KINGDOM OF GOD 18

CHAPTER 2. HOW TO ACCESS THE RESURRECTED KING 32

CHAPTER 3. A RIGHTEOUS & JUST FATHER THE FATHER'S DESIRE AND HIS PLEASURE 42

CHAPTER 4. THE FATHER'S HEART DESIRE AND PURPOSE IS TO GIVE HIS CHILDREN HIS KINGDOM 53

CHAPTER 5. THE CITIZENS OF THE KINGDOM 64

CHAPTER 6. THE KINGDOM LIFE IN BELIEVERS 75

CHAPTER 7. THE KINGDOM OF GOD; THE TRUE ESSENCE OF LIVING 84

CHAPTER 8. FULFILLING YOUR SPECIFIC ASSIGNMENT IN THE KINGDOM 98

CHAPTER 9. KINGDOM REPRESENTATIVES 112

CHAPTER 10. KINGDOM GENERALS 126

CHAPTER 11. THE EMERGENCE OF NEW
KINGDOM LEADERS 138

CHAPTER 12. UNDERSTANDING
SONS & SONSHIP 145

CHAPTER 13. THE CHURCH AND THE
KINGDOM 171

CHAPTER 14. THE FUTURE KINGDOM 181

MORE BOOKS BY KELAFO AND
SHALLAYWA COLLIE 188

INTRODUCTION

JESUS AS KING

Every great people are usually the product of good or great leaders. Leaders are the result of the correct head, the first leader, perhaps, the king in a Kingdom. Every Kingdom has a king, and in the Kingdom of Heaven, God is the king. God, the Creator, Maker, Lord, Healer, and so on is the personalized character of this divine being. He ruled in the Kingdom of man as their King. Neither enthroned, selected, elected, but always represented among us.

Make no mistake to ask or doubt different beings with a variety of knowledge and character, which are demonstrated as wickedness, hostility, hospitality, honesty, love, humility, care, compassion, and so on. Remember, we gave those "Expressions"(persons) these names in order to show good or bad, acceptable or unacceptable, social or antisocial, rewardable or defiant.

The will of the King and maker is that His purpose brings better to the land of the living. It is His will that humankind live in the knowledge of good, and in every understanding of His Word. The Kingdom of Heaven does not only sound beautiful but peaceful. Our father's will is that the peace and beauty in Heaven should be with us also on earth.

When Jesus was being questioned in the courts of the Pharisees, He gave little or no answer because He was being tried in a wrong courtroom. However, when He was tried before Pilate who represented Caesar as King, He gave an answer because it was a clash and class of kings and Kingdoms. In fact, as their custom was – to write the offenses of a crucified criminal upon him – Jesus' offense was that He professed Himself a king. The Bible says,

> *"Then, they led Jesus from Caiaphas to the Praetorium, and it was early morning. But they themselves did not go into the Praetorium, lest they should be defiled, but that they might eat the Passover. Pilate then went out to them and said, "What accusation do you bring against this Man?" They answered and said to him, "If He were not an evil-*

doer, we would not have delivered Him up to you." Then Pilate said to them, "You take Him and judge Him according to your law." Therefore the Jews said to him, "It is not lawful for us to put anyone to death," that the saying of Jesus might be fulfilled which He spoke, signifying by what death He would die. Then Pilate entered the Praetorium again, called Jesus, and said to Him, "Are You the King of the Jews?" Jesus answered him, "Are you speaking for yourself about this, or did others tell you this concerning Me?" Pilate answered, "Am I a Jew? Your own nation and the chief priests have delivered You to me. What have You done?" Jesus answered, "My kingdom is not of this world. If My kingdom were of this world, My servants would fight, so that I should not be delivered to the Jews; but now My kingdom is not from here." Pilate, therefore, said to Him, "Are You a king then?" Jesus answered, "You say rightly that I am a king. For this cause, I was born, and for this cause, I have come into the world, that I should bear witness to the truth. Everyone who is of the truth hears My voice." Pilate said to Him, "What is truth?" And when he had said this, he went out again to the Jews, and said to them, "I find no fault in Him at all. "But you have a custom that I should release someone to you at the Passover. Do you, therefore, want me to release to you the King of the Jews?" Then they all cried again, saying, "Not this Man, but Barabbas!" Now Barabbas was a robber" (John 18:28-40 NKJV)

King's Nature

Who do we call a King? You will agree with me that there are some qualities that you will see in a king that makes you know that he is a king. Whenever you see a King, there are certain qualities you see in him that makes you recognize him as a King. Even if a king's presence is not announced, some things around him will announce his presence. For example, when you see a king, there will be regal around him. His guards, his robe, will surround him, or his dressing will portray royalty, he will speak with authority and not with fear or timidity. All these qualities and some more will make a person to recognize a king no matter where you meet him. A king does not necessarily need to announce his presence; his charisma announces him.

There are a lot of Kings in the Bible who were very popular, but let's take a look at King Ahasuerus.

"Now it came to pass in the days of Ahasuerus (this was the Ahasuerus who reigned over one hundred and twenty-seven provinces, from India to Ethiopia), in those days when King Ahasuerus sat on the throne of his kingdom, which was in Shushan the citadel, that in the third year of his reign he made a feast for all his officials and servants— the powers of Persia and Media, the nobles, and the princes of the provinces being before him— when he showed the riches of his glorious kingdom and the splendor of his ex-

cellent majesty for many days, one hundred and eighty days in all." (Esther 1:1-4 NKJV)

King Ahasuerus was a very influential King in the Bible. He was the King who married Esther. He was a very renowned king. He ruled over 127-provinces from India to Ethiopia. He gave a feast that lasted for six months and all his officials, governors, and all nobles were in attendance. He was trying to impress his officials and I would like to imagine the amount of money that he must have spent. Of course, it will not be just a little amount of money. After those six months elapsed, He still gave orders for another seven days of feasting and this time, everyone was allowed to attend no matter who they were. Everyone drank from gold cups and everyone ate whatever they wanted. What an affluence! I want you to imagine the kind of affluence he displayed in his Kingdom, trying to show off to people the amount of power he possessed.

He portrayed the example of a king with affluence. He was a king that his presence does not need to be announced. No matter where he was, he would have stood out and would have looked highly influential.

God is king

When we speak about all these great and powerful earthly Kings, and we try to picture the kind of power and affluence that they possess, why do we

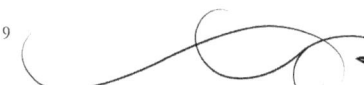

not try to know and understand the kind of power that Jesus has as the supreme King. We speak of great earthly kings today, without the knowledge of the fact that we have a king that is greater than them all. A king that supersedes all other kings; He is the King of Kings.

"And He has on His robe and on His thigh a name written: KING OF KINGS AND

LORD OF LORDS." (Revelations 19:16 NKJV)

David said in the book of Psalm **chapter 103 verses 19** that God has set His throne in Heaven, He rules over us all. He is the King! Many scriptures have established the Kingship of Christ and His Supremacy.

The Nature of Our King

The nature of kings refers to the characteristics or inherent qualities that they have that make them kings. This refers to things that we can see in them that make us recognize them as kings. Some of the qualities that we see in our earthly kings can also be identified with God, but in a different manner or approach.

When we see earthly kings, we recognize their supremacy, but they have limitations to their supremacy. Most times, most of those kings do not have a say when they leave their Kingdom, but Jesus has supremacy over all.

"God honored Jesus and lifted him high far beyond everything or anyone; so that all created things in heaven and on earth even those long ago dead and buried will bow in worship of Jesus Christ" (Philippians 2: 10 -11).

That is the supremacy of Christ. Jesus is a King and a ruler over all; everything in Heaven and on Earth. Jesus was given authority and supremacy everywhere and over everyone. Therefore, even though earthly kings have their supremacy, they are not able to express such supremacy everywhere. King Ahasuerus ruled over 127 provinces, he could not rule over all, but Jesus was given supremacy over everything on the whole earth.

In addition, when we see our earthly kings, we give them the respect they deserve, sometimes, we fear our kings. It is normal for every king to be greatly feared among his people, and so, even for our Jesus, the kind of honor that God has given Him is to make everyone in Heaven and on Earth to bow down wherever they hear His name. That is the kind of respect that was given to Jesus, that at the mention of His name, every knee should bow, and every tongue should confess that Jesus Christ is the Lord.

Earthly kings display a lot of affluence and are very wealthy, but our God is covered with such glory that we cannot even speak of or contain. His throne was described in ***Revelations chapter***

4 verse 1 through 10. Twenty-four elders would always bow down to give God all the glory. They will keep worshipping God forever and ever.

"After these things I looked, and behold, a door standing open in heaven. And the first voice which I heard was like a trumpet speaking with me, saying, "Come up here, and I will show you things which must take place after this." Immediately I was in the Spirit; and behold, a throne set in heaven, and One sat on the throne. And He who sat there was like a jasper and a sardius stone in appearance; and there was a rainbow around the throne, in appearance like an emerald. Around the throne were twenty-four thrones, and on the thrones, I saw twenty-four elders sitting, clothed in white robes; and they had crowns of gold on their heads. And from the throne proceeded lightnings, thunderings, and voices. Seven lamps of fire were burning before the throne, which are the seven Spirits of God. Before the throne, there was a sea of glass, like crystal. And in the midst of the throne, and around the throne, were four living creatures full of eyes in front and in back. The first living creature was like a lion, the second living creature like a calf, the third living creature had a face like a man, and the fourth living creature was like a flying eagle. The four living creatures, each having six wings, were full of eyes around and within. And they do not rest day or night, saying: "Holy, holy, holy, Lord God Almighty, Who was and is and is to come!" Whenever the living creatures give glory and honor and thanks to Him who sits on the throne, who lives forever and ever, the twenty-four elders fall down before Him who

sits on the throne and worship Him who lives forever and ever, and cast their crowns before the throne, saying: "You are worthy, O Lord, to receive glory and honor and power; For You created all things, and by Your will, they exist and were created." (Revelations 4:1-10 NKJV)

The King's Laws

Just as our earthly king's makes laws and give orders, Jesus gives us orders that we should follow. He gives us instructions about His Kingdom. One of the things He wants us to be able to do is to make us partakers in His Kingdom; He wants us to come and reign with Him.

> *"And there shall be no more curse, but the throne of God and of the Lamb shall be in it, and His servants shall serve Him. They shall see His face, and His name shall be on their foreheads. There shall be no night there: They need no lamp nor light of the sun, for the Lord God gives them light. And they shall reign forever and ever. Then he said to me, "These words are faithful and true." And the Lord God of the holy prophets sent His angel to show His servants the things which must shortly take place. "Behold I am coming quickly! Blessed is he who keeps the words of the prophecy of this book."* (Revelations 22: 3 – 7 NKJV)

Jesus tells us that His Kingdom is not a matter of eating and drinking, but righteousness and peace and joy in the Holy Ghost and that we are expected to follow the things, which make for peace and things.

"For the kingdom of God is not eating and drinking, but righteousness and peace and joy in the Holy Spirit. For he who serves Christ in these things is acceptable to God and approved by men. Therefore, let us pursue the things which make for peace and the things by which one may edify another." (Romans 14: 17 – 19 NKJV)

That is His law, that He has given us; to follow him, to seek for His Kingdom, and all other things shall be given to us.

Seeking the Kingdom First

God is first about man; therefore, man must be first about God. The Bible itself through the Lord Jesus Christ commanded man to seek first the Kingdom of God and His righteousness.

"But seek first the kingdom of God and His righteousness, and all these things shall be added to you." (Matthew 6:33 NKJV)

"He has shown you, O man, what is good; and what does the LORD require of you but to do justly, to love mercy, and to walk humbly with your God?" (Micah 6:8 NKJV)

According to God's design, the Kingdom must be a priority to man; and it has been made by God, such that success and fulfilment in life be hinged on the contribution of man to the Kingdom. The Kingdom must be first in a man's time, life, and family. One must ask himself or herself: why do I want to have the things I crave, like money, a marriage partner, time, cars, and even good health. Seeking after these things is not bad, but you must do so with the consciousness of priority. The things you seek, become relevant when you put the Kingdom of God first.

Seek the Kingdom First in Your Life

God is the source of life itself; therefore, the life of man must be for God. The Bible states that in Him we live, we move, and we have our being *(Acts 17:28).* Just as a fish dies when you take it outside the water, so also, a man dies when his life is lived outside God. This was like the story of Adam and Eve, who fell out of God's governance through the sin of disobedience. In the Kingdom of God, His glory sustains what is in it, but outside His governance, death reigns. Therefore, man's life and sustenance must be sourced in God.

Seek the Kingdom first with your time

The Psalmist wrote, *"… my times are in Thy hand." (Psalms 31:15).* It would be out of place for a man not to engage himself with things in such a way that he seems not to have time for His creator. God is a personality that manifests both outside times and in time, while man is only man because he is in time. Man must not prefer whiling away time to abiding in the presence of God; also, the entirety of man's purpose and destiny is factored into time, and therefore, does not have the whole of eternity to fulfil it. If a man must seek the Kingdom with his life, he must do so with his time!

Seek the Kingdom first with your family

God is the personality of the family. The Bible says,

> *"From whom the whole family I heaven and earth is named"* (Ephesians 3:15 NKJV).

When the Kingdom is sought after with the agency of the family being the subject, the family inadvertently adopts the Kingdom style of family living. This pattern is structured in such a way that man loves the wife as Christ loves the Church, the wife respects her husband according to the command of the Lord, and the children are brought upon in such a way that they exhibit the values of the Kingdom and even more. Isaiah tapped into this Kingdom vision of God when he uttered that *"I and the children that God has given me are for signs and wonders…"* (Isaiah 8:18); same as Joshua who said, *"…but as for me and my household, we shall serve the LORD"* (Joshua 24:15b)

Seeking the laws of the Kingdom in every decision

The Kingdom of God is such that laws back it up, and when decisions are based on these laws, they succeed because these laws are themselves backed by the integrity of God. The Bible says,

> *"Therefore whoever hears these sayings of Mine, and does them, I will liken him to a wise man who built his house on the rock: and the rain descended, the floods came, and the winds blew and beat on that house; and it did not fall, for it was founded on the rock."* (Matthew 7:24-25 NKJV)

The Gospel of the Kingdom is one that seeks to enthrone God as the King and His ideology in every stratum of human endeavor. Jesus said to His disciples; go into the entire world (the people, spheres of influence), and preach (proclaim, demonstrate) the gospel (a message with its ideology). The Gospel of the Kingdom is the one that ushers in the coming of the great King. **(Matthew 24:14).** The Gospel of the Kingdom is one that cries in reality, "Come Lord Jesus, and take your place."

CHAPTER ONE
THE MYSTERIES AND THE TRUTH OF THE KINGDOM OF GOD

The whole world is full of religion; in fact, the Church today is filled with so many religious people. At a point in time, I got tired of religion,- what this one and that one is saying, and I needed to go before the Lord to study this subject, which I had been studying for over twenty years; the Kingdom of God.

To reiterate , we need to know that what liberates men is not their commitment to religious activities, but the power of God, which is able to save and transform all men. The world is not going to be saved by viewing our religious activities; the world will only be convicted if they see the power of God.

The modern church is like a territory of confused individuals, who are exposed to different ideologies of God, and various doctrinal debates. So many ministries are rising, with various mandates and messages. However, it is obvious in the world today that people are hungry for the truth. A whole lot of folks are really searching for this truth because they are in bondage; many are under the oppression of devils. What truth are we supposed to share with them as believers?

There is no message that can change the world like the message of the Kingdom. It is the kingdom's message and the understanding of it that is capable of birthing change in the world. One important thing to note is that the church is the gateway through which people can be brought into God's Kingdom. The church is not a place of bondage where men should be tied to. Unfortunately, most of these folks in church, though active in church service have no relationship at all with Jesus. Painfully, many are only claiming to be working for the Lord, without even knowing the one they claim to be working for.

God has not called us out of darkness into bondage, he has actually called us into liberty, which means that we are not supposed to be bound by any religious law or belief system, we are actually supposed to be the representation of Jesus Christ, everywhere we find ourselves. The power of the Kingdom of God is not supposed to be limited to the confines of a church, but that every believer is successful in every aspect of their life. Believers should not just be celebrated for their success in church activities, but that every aspect of their life reveals the power of the Kingdom of God.

Revelation 12:7-10(NKJV):

"And war broke out in Heaven: Michael and his angels fought with the dragon; and the dragon and his angels fought, but they did not prevail, nor was a place found for them in Heaven any longer. So, the great dragon was cast out, that serpent of old, called the Devil and Satan, who deceives the whole world; he was cast to the earth, and his angels were cast out with him. Then I heard a loud voice saying in heaven, Now salvation, and strength, and the kingdom of our God, and the power of His Christ have come, for the accuser of our brethren, who accused them before our God day and night, has been cast down."

From the scripture above and other ones that will be cited later, we shall be identifying certain Kingdom mysteries.

1. Heaven is Real

Heaven is the place where God lives. Many people are made to believe that God lives in us, yes He does, but only by His Spirit; the geographical location where God resides and from where He governs the affairs of the universe is Heaven. In the scripture above, notice that there was war in Heaven because of the rebellious move of Lucifer. Unfortunately, for him, he lost his purpose because he stopped worshipping. He was then called; the dragon, the serpent, devil, and Satan. It is important to note that just as the Kingdom of Heaven signifies the residence of God, the Kingdom of God signifies the sovereignty of God.

Revelation 4:1-11(NKJV);

"After these things, I looked, and behold, a door standing open in heaven. And the first voice which I heard was like a trumpet speaking with me, saying, come up here, and I will show you things which must take place after this. Immediately I was in the Spirit; and behold, a throne set in heaven, and One sat on the throne. And He who sat there was like a jasper and a sardius stone in appearance; and there was a rainbow around the throne, in appearance like an emerald. Around the throne were twenty-four thrones, and on the thrones, I saw twenty-four elders sitting, clothed

in white robes; and they had crowns of gold on their heads. And from the throne proceeded flashes of lightning, thundering, and voices. Seven lamps of fire were burning before the throne, which are the seven Spirits of God. Before the throne, there was a sea of glass, like crystal. And in the midst of the throne, and around the throne, were four living creatures full of eyes in front and back. The first living creature was like a lion, the second living creature like a calf, the third living creature had a face like a man, and the fourth living creature was like a flying eagle. The four living creatures, each having six wings, were full of eyes around and within. And they do not rest day or night, saying: Holy, Holy, Holy, Lord God Almighty, Who was and is and is to come! Whenever the living creatures give glory and honor and thanks to Him who sits on the throne, who lives forever and ever, the twenty-four elders fall down before Him who sits on the throne and worship Him who lives forever and ever, and cast their crowns before the throne, saying: You are worthy, O Lord, to receive glory and honor and power; for You created all things, and by Your will, they exist and were created."

From the scripture above, one major point that can be deduced is that, one has to be in the Spirit to see Heaven; the same way one cannot access the Kingdom of God on earth without the Spirit of God.

Another thing to draw out is that, the permanent position of Jesus Christ in Heaven is KING. Of course, He is a healer, a deliverer, a savior, and many other good titles we can mention, hence, all of those offices become irrelevant once this world is over, simply because Jesus will not need to heal anyone in Heaven, there is no sickness there. There is no one to save or deliver in Heaven; it all ends here on earth. His permanent position in Heaven is King, and that is why He is called the King of Kings.

In the world system, there are certain places whereby certain offices are given the title Lord, most especially in the judiciary. Mind you, He is not just called King, by extension, He is also Lord, and He is the Lord of lords.

2. The Kingdom of Heaven is filled With Worship

> *Those who would be able to inherit the Kingdom of God and enter into the Kingdom of Heaven are the true worshippers*

One activity that goes on without a break in Heaven is worship. Notice how the twenty-four Elders bow down before His throne worshipping Him without a break. Heaven is a place of worship, and this is why God seeks worshippers on earth to worship Him in Spirit and in Truth. In fact, those who would be able to inherit the Kingdom of God and enter into the Kingdom of Heaven are the true worshippers, who will never be tired of worshipping God even in eternity.

3. There Are Beings in Heavens Created To Worship God

Even if no man is willing to worship, God is never starved of worship. Although, God cannot worship Himself, yet, there are beings created to give Him absolute worship without taking a break. We should not forget that Lucifer used to be one of them, if not the chiefest of them all, but just because he wanted to be god, he lost his place before God.

4. There is Holiness in the Kingdom of God

> *Holiness is a language and system of God's Kingdom.*

The words that come forth from the mouth of the twenty-four Elders as they worship are; "Holy, Holy, Holy, Lord God Almighty...." This proves that holiness is a language and system of God's Kingdom. It is imperative to note that that which is not Holy cannot see God, nor enter into the Kingdom of God. Holiness is one key that grants anyone access to the Kingdom of God.

It is also important to note that, holiness is not all about not committing sin, it is about being whole. If holiness was about not committing sin, then it simply means God is placing responsibility on us, a condition we might not be able to meet up with, in the flesh except by the help of the Holy Spirit. It is then important for us to understand that our righteousness is not vested in our ability not to sin, but in the power of Jesus Christ to save. In fact, there is nothing we can do by our self to make us righteous, for our righteousness is in Christ.

5. There is No Sin in God

Two words are connected to "Holiness," they are "faithfulness," and "integrity." Every believer needs to know that the faithfulness and the integrity of God can be trusted above everything else. God is not like men, He does not change; He is the same yesterday, today, and forever.

6. Jesus is Lord

Just as it was cited earlier, Jesus Christ is not only King, He is also Lord. The word "Lord," means "Sovereign ruler," or "owner." There may be other people called lord by virtue of their offices or governmental policies, hence, Jesus Christ is the Lord of lords; the Lord of all. If you are renting think of what the persons who own the premises is called – the Landlord.

As much as He is Lord to all, you as an individual must also have Him as your Lord. He must also be your Lord, not just the general office of a Lord, but your personal Lord. He is Lord to everyone, hence, you must understand this to the point that He becomes your Lord, you should be able to address Him as; "My Lord." If then you have been able to establish such a relationship with Him, you should be rest assured that you have to access to certain benefits, one of which is the fact that your resources come from Him. Hell is not supposed to be your experience, it is like the prison of the Kingdom, and it is meant for the devil and his cohorts.

7. There is No Beginning and End to the Kingship of Jesus

Jesus is King now, and He will remain King forever. He is not contesting to be Lord, He is already King and He alone is worthy to be Lord. Every good thing in existence belongs to Him. Every human in existence belongs to Jesus whether they are aware or not.

8. Jesus Christ is a Worthy Lord

In the world today, we celebrate men to the extent that we see them as worthy of being lord over us. Certain people are holding religious titles today, who men worship as lord. In fact, they lord themselves over others and demand certain privileges that may appear inhumane. But then, no matter what anyone has achieved, or the position that anyone has attained, they can't be lord overall, as they are also under the Lordship of Jesus Christ, the Lord of lords; the Lord of all.

Am I then suggesting that men should not be respected? Of course, men who deserve to be honored must be given the honor that is due to them without any form of exaggeration. Men should be respected, but not worshipped, Jesus alone is Lord; He alone deserves to be worshipped.

> *The Kingdom of God and the Kingdom of Heaven had been in existence from eternity, and will remain forevermore.*

Can I press further by saying, the Kingdom of God and the Kingdom of Heaven had been in existence from eternity, and will remain forevermore.

Psalm 45:6(NKJV):

"Your throne, O God, is forever and ever; a scepter of righteousness is the scepter of Your kingdom."

No matter what happens, no matter the heights of the persecution of the church, it is important to know that nobody can stop the Church. The Kingdom of God is unshakeable, no matter what happens, it stands forever!

Therefore, every believer needs to know they have to be eternally minded. Believers have to focus much more on things of eternal value, rather than chasing shadows right here on earth.

9. The Kingdom of God is Righteous

What this presupposes to mean is that there is equity in the Kingdom of God. This is not that kind of kingdom where certain men are segregated from others because of the color of their skin, or their age, or gender; it is a Kingdom where everyone is welcomed.

10. The Quicker You Change and Repent, The Quicker Your Miracle Comes

When the message of the Kingdom is brought to you and you are able to discover where you are not getting it right, what you are supposed to do next is to go before the Lord and repent from your resistance of the Kingdom all along. As soon as you realize where you had been wrong, and you confess your acceptance of the Kingdom of God, then, you begin to have access to the benefits of the Kingdom.

Psalm 145:10-13(NKJV);

"All Your works shall praise You, O Lord, and Your saints shall bless You. They shall speak of the glory of Your Kingdom, and talk of your power, to make known to the sons of men His mighty acts, and the glorious majesty of His Kingdom. Your Kingdom is an everlasting Kingdom, and Your dominion endures throughout all generations."

11. The Kingdom is full of Praise

Notice how the psalmist describes the attitude of praise in the Kingdom of God and Heaven. No one with the understanding of the Kingdom finds it difficult to give praise to God. No matter what the situation may be, praise is always in the mouth of anyone who is Kingdom-minded.

12. You are Going To be Eternal Like Your King

Just as Jesus is an eternal King and His Kingdom is an eternal Kingdom, you need to know that even when this present world is over, you would still be relevant in the Kingdom of your Father, giving Him the worship that He deserves forevermore.

Jesus, the King Himself, says a lot about His Kingdom;

"But, when He was alone, those around Him with the twelve asked Him about the parable. And He said to them, To you, it has been given to know the [d]mystery of the kingdom of God; but to those who are outside, all things come in parables, so that seeing, they may see and not perceive, and hearing they may hear and not understand; lest they should turn, and their sins be forgiven of them. *(Mark 4:10-12 NKJV)*

The deduction from the scripture above is that the Kingdom of Christ has mysteries, and those who do not make Jesus the Lord of their life will not understand the mysteries of the Kingdom.

Christ the King also made a fundamental point in (***Mark 10:13-15***)

"Then they brought little children to Him, that He might touch them; but the disciples rebuked those who brought them. But when Jesus saw it, He was greatly displeased and said to them, Let the little children come to Me, and do not forbid them; for of such is the kingdom of God. Assuredly, I say to you, whoever does not receive the Kingdom of God as a little child will by no means enter it."

It simply means anyone who intends to enter into the Kingdom of God must accept it as a child; the place of humility in accessing the Kingdom of God cannot be overemphasized.

What is the essence of the message or doctrine that we preach if the Kingdom of God is not duly emphasized? Just as Christ the King of this Kingdom preached the message of the Kingdom during His earthly ministry, it is therefore obligatory for every minister to emphasize on the message of the Kingdom of God and of Heaven.

Luke 4:43(NKJV);

"But He said to them, "I must preach the kingdom of God to the other cities also, because for this purpose I have been sent."

THE MYSTERIES AND THE TRUTH OF THE KINGDOM OF GOD

Chapter Reflections

- _____
  _____
  _____
  _____

- _____
  _____
  _____
  _____

- _____
  _____
  _____
  _____

CHAPTER TWO
HOW TO ACCESS THE RESURRECTED KING

*(**Mark 16:6**) - "And he saith unto them, be not affrighted: Ye seek Jesus of Nazareth, which was crucified: he is risen; he is not here: behold the place where they laid him."*

*The resurrection of Jesus Christ, the King of kings is the foundation of all Christian hope, and according to Apostle Paul, "…if Christ be not risen, then is our preaching vain, and your faith is also vain." (**I Corinthians 15: 14**).*

The new life which marks the beginning of the Christian life is the result of Christ's resurrection from the dead, for while the crucifixion of the Lord holds much stake in the redemption of man, His resurrection sealed the new life.

If the Lord had only died, but failed to rise again, then man wouldn't have had hope of eternal life, and there would have been no proof that Christ's sacrifice was accepted by God as a payment for man's sins.

This resurrection is the firm source of hope for all Kingdom pilgrims here on earth, as it's the reference point of the hope that believers have for resurrection, at the end of times.

In this chapter, we'll be considering how believers can claim the full benefits of Jesus's resurrection from the dead.

And to effectively outline this, we'll be breaking down the chapter into four sections:

- His Resurrection for Man's Redemption
- The Place of Faith in Accessing Jesus Christ
- Necessary Steps for Salvation
- The Priority of the Kingdom in our Lives

1. His Resurrection for Man's Redemption

All through the New Testament of the Bible, accounts of Christ's resurrection abound, and all these points to one thing, which is the redemption of man.

Man's redemption was planned by God since the fall of man, and the resurrection of Jesus Christ signified the activation of this plan.

We know that man sinned and fell from grace when the first man and woman disobeyed God. This sin brought about untold hardship upon man, and history is painted with horrible accounts of man's depravity and its grievous consequences. God's plan for man was never to destroy humanity, hence the time came when His only begotten Son had to be the price for man's restoration.

Man's redemption through Christ's resurrection is clearly exemplified by the following narrative.

When a man with debt dies, his debts are passed down to his children, and his entire estate. All that comes after this debtor is therefore constrained to be debtors themselves to the creditor, and until the debt is paid (or pardon is offered), they'll remain slaves for their generations.

However, when a worthy compensation is made for the debt, then those who've been under this bondage is totally freed, and are no more to be held responsible to the creditor for the old debt.

Now, the first man became a debtor to God when he rebelled against God's commandment by eating the forbidden fruit, and because he couldn't pay his debt, all his offspring (which accounts for the entire humanity) retained this debt upon them, and as the Bible says; in **Romans 3: 23:**

"For all have sinned, and come short of the glory of God."

Because man couldn't pay for his debts, his generations remained debtors for years, but when Jesus came, died, and rose again; he paid man's debts and obtained God's favour for man once again.

This verifies why Christ's resurrection is indispensable for the redemption of mankind.

The Place of Faith in Accessing Jesus Christ

"But without faith, it is impossible to please Him: for he that cometh to God must believe that He is, and that He is a rewarder of them that diligently seek Him."

(Hebrews 11:6)

The place of Faith in accessing the redemption that comes through Christ Jesus is non-negotiable, and to understand why this is so, every prospective Kingdom citizen must first realize what it means to have faith in God.

Now, the Bible defines faith as the substance of things hoped for, the evidence of things not seen. **[Hebrews 11:1]**. This means that faith is actually the practice of believing something that apparently has no physical evidence, that is – something, which cannot be seen by the eyes, cannot be heard by the ears, and cannot be touched by the physical body.

Faith, therefore, implies, stepping beyond the realms of the physical, into the realms of the supernatural.

So, why is faith the all-important factor for accessing this redemption that comes through Christ?

Faith is indispensable because this redemption that we speak about is not physical. It's not a price being paid to a physical being, rather it is being paid to God.

Moreover, the actual transaction that bought man this redemption was not physical as no man saw when the Lord Jesus went down to the grave and conquered the powers of sin and death. This we all believe by faith, having seen reason for it to be true that as Christ Jesus came, for this reason, died, and rose for this reason.

> *This faith then demands that we accept our natural sinfulness, believe that Jesus has paid the price for us*

Therefore by faith, we believe that Christ died and rose again, and have paid the price for our redemption. This faith then demands that we accept our natural sinfulness, believe that Jesus has paid the price for us, confess our sins, and confess the Lord Jesus to be our saviour. Then by faith, we trust to have obtained forgiveness from God and grace to become Kingdom citizens.

2. Necessary Steps for Salvation

How then can one be saved and accepted into God's Kingdom?

The Bible records in *(Acts 2: 38)*, the answer Apostle Peter made to the men who asked him the question above. It was the eve of the day of Pentecost when the Holy Spirit first descended on the church, the effect of this infilling had spurred the Apostle to preach the word so boldly to those who were gathered around. The Bible records that conviction fell on these men, and they asked for the way of Salvation. Below is the answer given to them by the Apostle.

Acts 2:38 - *"Then Peter said unto them, Repent, and be baptized every one of you in the name of Jesus Christ for the remission of sins, and ye shall receive the gift of the Holy Ghost."*

This leads us to the sure steps to Salvation.

> *Repentance is indispensable for Salvation*

Repentance: Everyone who wishes to access salvation through Jesus Christ, must realize and accept that he/she is a sinner, and must repent from his/her sins. Repentance is indispensable for Salvation, and it includes the confession of such sins to God in prayer.

Believe in Christ's Resurrection: According to ***Romans 10: 9***, belief in Christ's resurrection is indispensable to accessing the Salvation that comes through Christ. For one to be saved, he/she must believe that Christ is risen from the dead.

Believe and Trust the Grace of God: By grace, we are saved, through faith – and not by our own works. This is what the Bible says in (***Ephesians 2: 8***) Hence for anyone to be saved and sustained in the faith, he/she must believe in God's grace and trust this sufficient grace of God to be able to keep him/her in the faith.

Summarily, the steps to Salvation are; Repentance, Believing in Christ's Resurrection, and Trust in God's grace. With these in place, one's salvation is sure, and such a person is granted access to God's Kingdom.

3. The Priority of the Kingdom in our Lives

Finally, what's the priority of the Kingdom in our lives? And why must we prioritize the kingdom of God?

(Matthew 6: 33) says:

"But seek ye first the kingdom of God, and his righteousness; and all these things shall be added unto you."

The priority of the Kingdom is not negotiable for every Kingdom citizen, this is quite because it's the one factor that proves our true allegiance to the King. One cannot claim to be committed to the things of God if he/she or she is preoccupied with the things of the world.

Many Christians/Kingdom citizens claim to prioritize the Kingdom of the Heavenly king in their daily living, but a clear observation proves they actually don't do that. They instead live their lives in ways that prioritize the things of this world, so the question goes; what does it mean to prioritize the Kingdom?

- To prioritize the Kingdom means that we wake up each morning seeking to know and do the will of God.

- To prioritize the kingdom means that we avoid activities that tend to sin, and which do not glorify God.

- To prioritize the kingdom means that we consistently commit to preaching the Gospel, as commanded by the Lord Jesus

- Finally, to prioritize the Kingdom means we forsake all the pleasures and treasures of this world and run towards the Heavenly Jerusalem, the city of our King.

More than ever before, the King beckons us to commit more to the Kingdom, and once we do so, He won't relent in availing us the unlimited riches of the Kingdom. Remember Jesus has paid all our dues, and all we need to do is gratefully accept His offer and live in the fullness of it.

Chapter Reflections

- _____
  _____
  _____

- _____
  _____
  _____
  _____

- _____
  _____
  _____

CHAPTER THREE
A RIGHTEOUS & JUST FATHER THE FATHER'S DESIRE AND HIS PLEASURE

Praise the Lord we have looked at the nature, qualities and character of our Father briefly in the first few chapters. Our Father is absolutely wonderful, mighty, holy, pure, righteous, just and loving to name a few traits. He is so much more than words can even describe. He is established on a throne of majesty and dominion; He is the image of God seen in the life of Jesus Christ and yet He is also the sweet, gentle, passionate Holy Spirit. Our Father is a mighty ruler who has dominion and power over the visible and invisible world; yet He has His children constantly on His mind. He made all provisions through the shed blood of Christ to save and restore man to relationship with the Father. He made us co-heirs and co-rulers over the affairs of the Father's Kingdom in the earth.

> *He is established on a throne of majesty and dominion*

Let us now explore the desires and pleasures of our Father. Yes He is King and a judge but He is also very passionate about fulfilling some of His most intimate dreams and visions also. Consider that concept and imagine? What an amazing delight that would be for us as humans to assist in the mighty King's desires.

Wow! Firstly, let's explore some of His pleasures.

He Desires Worship

In a brief encounter with a Samaritan woman, at a well in a city called Samaria, Jesus outlines the new order for the reverence and the giving of credit to the Father. Jesus asked a woman of another race, as Jew, to give Him water. It was not a custom foe interaction with this woman a Samaritan and a Jew.

However, Jesus being the express image and fullness of the nature of our heavenly father intentionally crosses the humanity erected walls of sep-

aration and lovingly touches the disheartened soul of an emotional detach woman. This woman was in search of an identity and a heritage.

Jesus gently orchestrates the woman into relationship to her source, her Father through teaching her about what the Father really longs for. He longs for a pure heart giving worship from His children! He loves praises of sincerity, thanksgiving and honour that are wrapped in reverence in to who He is.

John 4:21 *"Jesus saith unto her, Woman believe me, the hour cometh, when ye shall neither in this mountain, not yet at Jerusalem, worship the Father," Jesus is removing the geographical form of worship only and establishing a worship that can occur anywhere, at any time."*

(vs. 22) *"Ye worship ye know not what: we know what we worship: for salvation is of the Jews."*

(vs. 23) *"But the hour cometh and now is when the true worshippers shall worship the Father in spirit and in truth: for the Father seeketh such to worship him."*

Amazing, the Father seeks for persons to worship Him in Spirit and in truth.

The scriptures record that the eyes of the Lord seeketh to and fro for worshippers in the earth. It also outlines that He dwells in the praises of His people. He come down and becomes enthroned in our midst.

Psalm 22:3 *"But thou art holy, O thou, that inhabits the praises of Israel."*

Psalm 145:1 *"I will extol thee, my God, O king; and I will bless thy name forever and ever."*

(vs. 2) *"Every day will I bless thee; and I will praise thy name forever and ever."* **(vs. 3)** *"Great is the Lord, and greatly to be praised; and His great-ness is unsearchable."* **(vs. 4)** *"One generation shall praise thy works to another, and shall declare thy mighty acts."* **(vs. 5)** *"I will speak of the glorious honour of thy majesty, and of thy wondrous works."*

(vs. 6) *"And men shall speak of the might of thy terrible acts: and I will declare thy greatness."*

(vs. 10) *"All thy works shall praise thee, O Lord; and thy saints shall bless thee."*

(vs. 11) *"They shall speak of the glory of thy kingdom, and talk of thy power;*

(vs. 12) *"To make known to the sons of men his mighty acts, and the glorious majesty of His Kingdom."* **(vs. 13)** *"Thy kingdom is an everlasting kingdom, and thy dominion endureth throughout all generations."*

Daddy's Delight

Psalm 35:27 *"Let them shout for joy, and be glad that favor my righteous cause: yea, let them say continually, Let the Lord be magnified, which hath pleasure in the prosperity of his servant."*

Our daddy has a few secrets about Him that as a Son, I will reveal to the other family members. He has pleasures, He enjoys certain things and we are going to explore those areas. The King loves to be pleasured by His creation.

Earlier we saw that daddy loves worship and praise not only from His creation but also from humans. He sings over us and we sing unto Him. Our Father does not need to be any bigger than He is; but He loves when we honour and adore Him by our own free will. He loves when we acknowledge as humans that He is the source of our very existence! He is jealous over our worship and adoration. He knows that our worship establishes the knowledge that we did not create ourselves and that we must fully trust Him. As a King who has lordship over His subjects who are also His children; our worship obliges the Father to provide, protect and sustain us Hallelujah!!

He also has pleasures to be received. The word pleasure from the Hebrew gives a clear picture of His emotional nature. The *Lexical Aids* to the Old Testament **'Chaphets'** (2654) means to:

1.) "To take delight in.

2.) Be pleased with.

3.) Have affection for...

4.) To desire, like...

5.) To feel a strong positive attraction for something."

Our Father has strong desires and affections. The next few words truly impressed me. Usually a person would have a desire for a particular food such as icecream, a favourite television show or movie. For example even a particular fragrance or colour. However our God desires to see His children prosper. Wow!

Our Father sits on His throne and longs for a sincere passion to see His children increase in every area of their lives. He is constantly talking, instructing, directing and ordering the necessary plans needed them. He gets enjoyment when His sons inherit every promise and goodness in their lives and the live to come.

James 1:17 *"Every good gift and every perfect gift is from above, and cometh down from the Father of lights with whom is no variableness, neither shadow of turning."*

This scripture brilliantly expounds that all good things are those made available by the hand of the Father. The gift of life, health, liberty, strength to achieve goals, the right connections of persons to propel us into our destiny, He strategically sets in order. In fact our Father allows the rain, or the goodness of life to be made available to the just and unjust person. He so loves that He allows His good nature and resources to be given to those who do love Him and refuse to honour Him. What a loving Father!

The word prosperity (7965) comes from the Hebrew 'Shalom' (*Lexical Aids* to the Old Testament). **1)** 'Shalom' means health, security, tranquillity, welfare and good condition. This word carries the embodiment success, comfort, peace, whole, secure, safe, happy and sound. **2)** A state of well-being. The *reference dictionary* depicts shalom "as a satisfied condition, an unconcerned state of peacefulness. **'Shalom'** is a harmonious state of soul and mind both externally and internally. The writer states in the *Lexical Aids* that to wish one shalom implies a blessing.

The root word of Shalom is Shalam (7999) meaning to be whole, to be sound, be safe, to keep safe, to make secure, and to live in harmony with God. God our father sits in the heavenlies and has a sincere passion to see the health of His children. The Scripture records a number of interesting outlines that expresses this concern the Father has for the physical well-being of His people. Health describe by most dictionaries or reference books 'is the state of well-being, physically, mentally, emotionally, and spiritually and not just the absence of disease.'

He says I am the Lord that healeth your diseases and another place the scripture records in **Isaiah**

53:5 *"But He was wounded for our transgressions He was bruised for our iniquities: the chastisement of our peace was upon Him; and with His stripes we are healed."*

Our Father does not only want His people to receive divine supernatural healing but walk in a continuous flow of the anointing of health. The Father has made provision already by the shed blood of Jesus Christ. We have the right and the Father's sincere passion to walk whole.

> *walk in a continuous flow of the anointing of health*

Therefore, reject every illness and disease that tries to manifest in the body of your family or your life. Stand on the "Shalom" word spoken over your life. Stand up in the father's desire for your life and allow His word to line up with your body and mind. This health also encompasses the mental well-being of His children. Daddy delights when His children can rest and sleep stress free. He wants comfort in the time of trouble.

Isaiah 26:3-4 *"Thou wilt keep him in perfect peace, whose mind is stayed on thee: because he trusteth in thee.*

(vs. 4) *"Trust ye in the Lord forever: for in the Lord JEHOVAH is everlasting strength."*

He will maintain our complete soundness and peace if we remember His heart's desire and plan for us to continually be whole in our mind. Jesus

expresses emphatically in Matthew's account of the Gospel Jesus' desire, the Father's heart that His Sons walk in the mental peace and wholeness amidst any challenging or distressing situations.

Matthew 11:28 *"Come unto me, all ye that labour and are heavy laden, and I will give you rest."* **(vs. 29)** *"Take my yoke upon you, and learn of me; for I am meek, and lowly in heart: and ye shall find rest unto your souls."*

There is a place of rest or settling when we turn to Jesus Christ. And again the word records, **Psalm 127:2** *"It is vain for you to rise up early, to sit up late, to eat the bread of sorrows: for so He giveth His beloved sleep."*

Well, let us examine our Father's thought's concerning His Sons under the desires of the Papa. **Psalm 139:17** *"How precious also are thy thoughts unto me, O God! How great is the sum of them!"*

(vs. 18) *"If I should count them, they are more in numbers than the sands: when I awake, I am still with thee."*

His mind is filled with the wonders of how He is going to bless us. They are so numerous they would compare with the amount of sand on seashore. He thinks about the complete wholeness of His children. Praise God!!!

Chapter Principles

- Our Father is holy pure, righteous and is a just King.

- Our Heavenly Father desires the act of worship. Worship is the act of giving value to something of significant worth.

- A King as our Father desires honour, praise, thanks and worship from His subjects.

- Worship is and act fitting to one whom has power over your life and all creation. Our father is a King deserving of honour.

- Our Father delights in the prosperity of His people. He wants His sons to be successful.

- Our Father desire's the 'Shalom' complete wholeness of life to be the model of His children's lives.

Chapter Reflections

- _____
  _____
  _____

- _____
  _____
  _____

- _____
  _____
  _____

CHAPTER FOUR
THE FATHER'S HEART DESIRE AND PURPOSE IS TO GIVE HIS CHILDREN HIS KINGDOM

The Father has an unselfish heart and deep passion to enter into an eternal partnership with His sons in the management of all His Kingdom. Daddy wants to entrust sons as trustees in the earth and marketplaces to establish righteous rule and laws in all arenas of humanly interaction. Even more glorious is that He also wants to entrust His sons as heirs with God and co-heir in the rule and reign in the Kingdom to come. Praise God!!

One writer profoundly articulates that a wise father leaves an inheritance for His children and children's children. Our heavenly Father is the prototype of the fatherhood and does the exact same principle of giving an inheritance to His children. He gives the inheritance to His children and generations thereafter. He gives the inheritance of <u>identity</u>, <u>ownership</u>, <u>rule ship</u>, <u>partnership</u> and <u>fellowship</u> to His Sons.

Let us examine those concepts briefly from the scriptures account of God's inheritance to man.

Genesis 1:26 *"And God said, let us make man in our image, after our likeness: and let them have dominion over the fish of the sea, and over the cattle, and over all the earth and over every creeping thing that creepeth upon the earth."*

(vs. 27) *"So God <u>created</u> man in His own image, in the image of God created he him, <u>male</u> and <u>female</u> created He them."*

(vs. 28) *"And God blessed them and God said unto them, be fruitful, and multiply, and replenish the earth and subdue it and have dominion over the fish of the sea, and over the fowl of the air, and over every living thing that moveth upon the earth."*

(vs. 29) *"And God said, Behold, I have given you every herb bearing seed, which is upon the face of all the earth and every tree yielding seed; to you it shall be meat."*

There are astounding relations locked into these few verses in which many great generals in the body of Christ have unlocked over the ages. Many have uncovered the original intent of God for man, the ruler ship authority and position of man; the delegated stewardship of man over the earth and its resources.

For this book purpose let us examine **Genesis 1:26-30:**

1. Image of Mankind.

2. Dominion of Mankind.

3. Ownership of Mankind.

4. Empowered to prosper by God over humanity.

Our Father like any other earthly male usually wants to continue His seed and lineage throughout the generations. Our Father did that by forming man with His spiritual DNA. Enclose within every human being is the genetic code of their father. In science the genetic code can be divided into the genotype and the phenotype. Scientist we concur that the genotype is not always seen in the physical outside appearance of an offspring. This means that by simply looking at a species it is not obvious at times that it came from a particular parent. Hence, a complex study has to be taken from a species, for example a blood sample, analysed and genetic code determined. However, the phenotype is the external physical characteristic that portrays the features of its parent's appearance. For example, a person's blood, hair, along with other distinct features of its parents in humans.

This analogy represents the offspring of the heavenly Father; there are many who don't have the express image and nature of the Father through Jesus Christ. Yet there are those who not only carry the concealed DNA of the Father but also express the nature, love, character authority and dominion of Him.

John 4:24 states that *"God is a spirit..."*

Hence man being in the image and likeness of God must be a spirit and merely possess a spirit. The Father then gives man dominion of Kingdom rule over the earth and its creatures.

The dominion man was given best be interpreted from *Lexical Aids* to the Old Testament 7287 **('Radah') meaning to 'tread down' (as a wine press, with the feet); to subjugate, subdue.**

It also expresses the meaning, **to crumble, rule, cause to rule, have reign over and prevail against.** Hence, the Father created man with the same nature as He is being a King and Lord, full with authority, power, and ruler ship. He then gives man the territory to reign based on the fore knowledge that the essence of governance is in man. He is aware that man's genetic code enables them to subdue life and manage the resources of earth. The Father moves into a greater love support by proclaiming and empowering man to prosper.

Genesis 1:28 *"And God blesses them, and God said unto them, "Be fruitful and multiply and replenish the earth and subdue it."*

The Father extended His favour, grace and release of goodness to flow on the life of His first created son Adam and his offspring. He commanded His sons to bring about increase harvest replication of all that is with the Godly essence in man and cause it to manifest and fill the earth. His sons were to then govern the products of man's invention, the earth and environment in accordance with the laws and nature of our righteous Father and King.

Daniel, the prophet hundreds of years after the relinquishing of man's dominion to Satan recalls the original intent of the Father in:

Daniel 7:18 *"But the saints of the Most High shall take the Kingdom, and possess the Kingdom forever, even forever and ever."*

Daniel 7:27 *"And the Kingdom and dominion, and the greatness of the Kingdom under the whole heaven, shall be given to the people of the saints of the Most High, whose Kingdom is an everlasting Kingdom, and all dominions shall serve and obey Him."*

Exodus 19:5 *"Now therefore, if ye will obey my voice indeed, and keep my covenant, then ye shall be a peculiar treasure unto me above all people: for all the earth is mine:"*

(vs. 6) *"And ye shall be unto me a kingdom of priests, and a holy nation. These are the words which thou shalt speak unto the children of Israel."*

The Father clearly expresses through the vision and prophecies to Daniel the sons of the Most High will possess the Kingdom. The term the prophet used is the word *"saints;"* this does not refer to a selected group of persons who an organization defined.

Contrary, according to the *Lexical Aids* to the Old Testament saint (6922) means **Qadosh (6918) and Qadash (6942)**.'**Qadosh**' means sacred, selected, pure, holy, consecrated, and pious.

Hence the concept is a group of persons set aside, consecrated unto the purpose and calling of the Heavenly Father. The Father's Holy sons, who have separated themselves unto the work, character and obedience to the Father, will possess the Kingdom of God.

'**Q"d"sh**' **(**6942) express a similar meaning to be hallow, dedicated, holy, purify and consecrated to God. It signifies an act or a state in which people or things are set aside for use in the worship of God. Therefore the mature Sons who have continuous obedience and fellowship with the Father will inhabit the Kingdoms.

The Old Testament definition of the Kingdom the saints will possess is derived from the Hebrew '**malkût**' (4438),

Kingdom; reign and rule.

The word denotes **1.)** The territory of the Kingdom. **2.)** The accession to the throne. **3.)** Anything Royal or Kingly.

Lexical Aids to the Old Testament describes (**'malkhuth'**– 4438) as a dominion, an empire a Kingdom, a realm, a reign, royal rule and sovereign power. 'Malkhuth' comes from the noun 'M!lakh' (4427) meaning to be King. The essential understanding of M!lakh is exercising the functions of a monarchy or royal authority. M!lakh can be the act of God or men in exalting a person to the office of royalty.

Hence the concept of the father giving His Sons a territory in which they can exercise kingly rule and sovereign power to govern other words that expresses the Father's desire for His children is the words from *Vines Complete Expository Dictionary*: *Basileia* (Kingship; Kingdom; royal power). Another translation of the kingdom is the words **mamil"k"h** (4467) signifies **kingdom, sovereignty; dominion; reign.**

The basic meaning of *'manil!k!h'* is the area and people that constitute a Kingdom. It can also be synonym nouns to nation. Manil!k!h can also denotes, "Kings" as the king was considered to be the embodiment of the "Kingdom."

The Old Testament further defines as expressions of the royal "rule" all things associated with the king:

Throne:

The throne expresses the symbolic head of the state, territory, royal rule and governance over a territory. It is a seat of power, influence and wealth and our Heavenly Father wants to give His rule over the natural and spiritual realm to His obedient Sons- Praise Jesus!

Luke 12:32 *"Fear not little flock; for it is your Father's good pleasure to give you the Kingdom."*

Jesus confirms to the disciples and spoke into the lives of the sons throughout the ages who sometimes become concerned about daily living.

The descriptions "Father's good pleasure" unlocks the fervent love and concern, daddy has for His children. The term according to *Lexical Aids* to the New Testament is **Eudok#$ (2106)** from **eu** well good and **dek#$** to think something good; not merely an understanding of what is right and good but stressing the willingness and freedom of an intention or resolve regarding what is good."

Here we understand that the Father extends benevolence, a gracious purpose to give His sons the royal ruler ship over the works He created. Hallelujah to our Father!

Chapter Principles

- The Father desires to establish His dominion ruler-ship in the earth under the entire universe is under the entire universe is under His righteous influence.

- The Father wants His righteous influence to reign and rule in the earth.

- The Kingdom of God is activated in any person through acceptance of Jesus Christ as 'Lord'.

- The Holy Spirit is sent as the promise to the believer in Jesus Christ. The Holy Spirit connects the communication between heaven and earth.

- The Holy Spirit works to mature infants in the faith to adult Sons

- Matured Sons execute the Father's will purpose and agenda in the earth partnering with the Holy Spirit.

- Sons are saints (selected, consecrated, set apart individuals.)

- It is the Father's good pleasure to give His children His Kingdom.

The Father's Heart Desire and Purpose is To give His children His Kingdom

Chapter Reflections

-
-
-

CHAPTER FIVE
THE CITIZENS OF THE KINGDOM

"Now, therefore, ye are no more strangers and foreigners, but fellow-citizens with the saints, and of the household of God," - Ephesians 2:19

Every nation or country has citizens, and the citizens of every Nation are distinguished by either their culture or language. If an Indian or Chinese comes to America, you will be able to tell that this fellow is not from America, because of his or her culture and language. In the same way, if an American goes to Eastern Europe, the people will also tell that such a person is coming from America, due to his or her language and culture.

Citizens of the Kingdom of God are called to a Holy and Heavenly lifestyle. It's important that we understand who we are as the citizens' of the Kingdom of God. This is because, there are many people who might be carrying themselves as citizens of the Kingdom of God, but in reality, they are strangers before God. We might see such people in our churches, or prayer meetings, but Heaven does not recognize them.

> *A citizen of a nation that does not know his or her right will face oppression*

More than that, it is important that we recognize the privileges and opportunities that every citizen in the Kingdom of God Have. A citizen of a nation that does not know his or her right will face oppression and denial of opportunities that should have been for him or her. There are privileges for every citizen of the Kingdom of God, and it is as we recognize them that they will be able to benefit us.

The allegiance or loyalty of every citizen is demanded. When a citizen refuses to pledge his or her allegiance to the laws of the country, his or her citizenship is revoked and such person is declared a "Persona non grata." Such a principle applies in the Kingdom of God. Allegiance is demanded, and when it is not given, some consequences will surely follow up. These are the things that we must understand as citizens of the Kingdom of God.

Who Are The Kingdom Citizens

The first thing that we must do is to understand whom and who are the citizens' of the Kingdom of God. Anyone can claim to be a citizen, but not everyone carries a heavenly passport. Jesus Christ said in (**Matthew 7:21**), *"Not everyone that saith unto me, Lord, Lord, shall enter into the kingdom of heaven; but he that doeth the will of my Father which is in Heaven."* It was important that Jesus clarifies the issue of whom and who will enter the Kingdom of God. This is because, on the last day, many will say to him, *"Lord, Lord, have we not prophesied in thy name? And in thy name have cast out devils? And in thy name done many wonderful works?"* (Matthew 7:22) He emphasized that only those who do the Will of God are the citizens of the Kingdom of God.

From the Old Testament, God has always given the requirement for citizenship in His Kingdom. When the children of Israel sinned in the wilderness by worshiping Baal, God told Moses in (**Exodus 32:33**) *"Whosoever hath sinned against me, him will I blot out of my book."* This shows us that there is a register that contains the names of the citizens of the Kingdom of God. Just as we have a database in our country, that contains the details of every citizen, there is also a database in Heaven that contains the details of every citizen of the Kingdom of God.

Who then are the citizens of the Kingdom of God? The citizens of the Kingdom of God are those whose sins have been washed by the blood of Jesus Christ the Son of God, and who believes and accepts Jesus Christ as the Lord and Saviour of his or her life. These people are those who have repented of their sins, renounced their past lives, and rejected every enticement to sin. Just as the Bible said in (**Galatians 2:20**), their confession always is *"I am crucified with Christ: nevertheless I live; yet not I, but Christ liveth in me: and the life which I now live in the flesh I live by the faith of the Son of God, who loved me, and gave himself for me."* They live a life of faith in God through Jesus Christ, and have surrendered all to Him. The Bible said in (**John 1:12**), *"But as many as received Him, to them gave He power to become the sons of God, even to them that believe on his name."* Citizens of the Kingdom of God are those who have received Jesus Christ into their hearts, and believe also on His name.

We were not born as citizens of the Kingdom of God. It was by the coming of Jesus Christ, and through His death on the cross that He procured our citizenship for us. (**Ephesians 2:12**) said, *"That at that time ye were without Christ, being aliens from the commonwealth of Israel, and strangers from the covenants of promise, having no hope, and without God in the world."* Before the coming of Christ into our hearts, we were aliens and strangers before God, but as Christ came, the Bible said in (***Ephesians 2:13***), "*But now in Christ Jesus ye who sometimes were far off are made nigh by the blood of Christ.*" The death of Christ made it possible for one to become a citizen of this Kingdom, and the Bible said in (***Ephesians 2:19***), "*Now, therefore, ye are no more strangers and foreigners, but fellow-citizens with the saints, and of the household of God;*" In summary, only those who have accepted Christ into their lives, and are living a life of obedience are called citizens of the Kingdom of Heaven.

Citizens of the Kingdom of God are called to live a separate and different life. They are sanctified for God, and called to be Holy. (***2 Corinthians 6:14-18***) tells us that they are not to be unequally yoked together with sinners. It said, "*Be ye not unequally yoked together with unbelievers: for what fellowship hath righteousness with unrighteousness? And what communion hath light with darkness? And what concord hath Christ with Belial? Or what part hath he that believeth with an infidel? And what agreement hath the temple of God with idols? For ye are the temple of the living God; as God hath said, I will dwell in them, and walk in them; and I will be their God, and they shall be my people. Wherefore come out from among them, and be ye separate, saith the Lord, and touch not the unclean thing; and I will receive you, And will be a Father unto you, and ye shall be my sons and daughters, saith the Lord Almighty.*" People who are citizens of the Kingdom of God obey the commandments of God, and will not soil their white garments through unequal yoke with the world. Thus, you must examine yourself and ask yourself if you are a citizen of the Kingdom of God.

The Allegiance of the Kingdom Citizens

Citizens of every nation pledge to serve and honor their country. Most countries say; "The Pledge" of their nation on every major occasion. This is to remind the citizens of their responsibility to honour and defend the nation.

Citizens of the Kingdom of God are to swear allegiance to Jesus Christ and Him alone. No one is to compete for attention in his or her hearts. Jesus Christ is Lord and Master of everything that they have. In the early church, despite persecution, the Bible said in (**Acts 5:29**), *"Then Peter and the other apostles answered and said, we ought to obey God rather than men."* These men were ready to lay down their lives for Christ till the end, without fear of what the persecutor might do.

The allegiance of the citizens of the Kingdom to Christ is forever. It is not an allegiance that expires after a while, once it expires, they lose their citizenship. The citizens are to swear allegiance to Christ as servants do to their masters. In (**Exodus 21:5, 6**), *"And if the servant shall plainly say, I love my master, my wife, and my children; I will not go out free:*

Then his master shall bring him unto the judges; he shall also bring him to the door, or unto the door post; and his master shall bore his ear through with an annul; and he shall serve him forever." A citizen that loves God will say beyond and more than what this servant said. He or she will also say "*I love my master, I will not go out free*" This will cause such an individual to dedicate his life to serve Christ forever.

> *Citizens of the kingdom of God are called to be servants of Christ.*

Citizens of the Kingdom of God have been bought with a price. The Bible said in **(1 Corinthians 6:19, 20)**, "*What? Know ye not that your body is the temple of the Holy Ghost which is in you, which ye have of God, and ye are not your own? For ye are bought with a price: therefore glorify God in your body, and in your spirit, which are God's.*" They can't do what they want, go to places they want, be anything that they want to be, no, they cannot. Everything that they are to do, must be according to the Word of God. They are to glorify God in everything that they do in order to show forth their allegiance to Him. Therefore, if what an individual is doing does not glorify God, such a person is not showing allegiance to Christ. **(1 Corinthians 7:23)** said, "*Ye are bought with a price; be not ye the servants of men.*" Citizens of the kingdom of God are called to be servants of Christ.

The Citizens and Their Privileges

Citizens of the kingdom of God are blessed with many privileges and opportunities. These privileges cannot be enjoyed by people who are yet to receive Christ. Of course, you can remember the story of the Syrophoenician woman who came to Jesus for her daughter's deliverance and healing. Jesus told her in (***Mark 7:27***) *"...Let the children first be filled: for it is not meet to take the children's bread, and to cast it unto the dogs."* He meant by this statement that healing was only for the children of the Kingdom.

The privileges of the citizens of the Kingdom are many and they include the following:

- **Prayer:** Prayer is a great privilege that every citizen has. It is the ability to communicate with God and to receive divine answers and help. The Bible said in (***Proverbs 15:8***) *"The sacrifice of the wicked is an abomination to the LORD: but the prayer of the upright is his delight."* God is always looking for His citizens to pray to Him, and when they pray, He will answer.

- **Protection:** Those who come under the leadership of God enjoy His protection. (***Psalms 91:1, 2***) said, "He *that dwelleth in the secret place of the Most High shall abide under the shadow of the Almighty. I will say of the LORD, He is my refuge and my fortress: my God; in Him will I trust."* Those who are not under God's shelter are prone to the devil's attack and onslaught.

- **Prosperity:** There is prosperity for those in the Kingdom of God because God has provided everything that is needed for life and godliness. *(**Psalms 122:7**)* said, *"Peace be within thy walls, and prosperity within thy palaces."* And in Psalms 35:27, it said, *"Let them shout for joy, and be glad, that favour my righteous cause: yea, let them say continually, Let the LORD be magnified, which hath pleasure in the prosperity of his servant."* God desires that everyone in His Kingdom prospers, in both spirit, soul, and body.

- **Power:** Citizens of the Kingdom of God have power at their disposal. Jesus Christ said in *(**Luke 10:19**)*, *"Behold, I give unto you power to tread on serpents and scorpions, and over all the power of the enemy: and nothing shall by any means hurt you."* Power is given to every citizens of the Kingdom of God because, *"God hath not given us the spirit of fear; but of power, and of love, and of a sound mind."* (2 Timothy 1:7) There is power available over the devil and his demons.

- **Peace:** Peace is something that the world does not have. No matter how they try, the kingdoms of this world can never have peace, but in the kingdom of God, there is peace. Jesus said in *(**John 14:27**)*, *"Peace I leave with you, my* *peace I give unto you: not as the world giveth, give I unto you. Let not your heart be troubled, neither let it be afraid."* There is peace in times of trouble and crisis. The world might be in chaos, but citizens of the kingdom have abundant peace. (**Isaiah 26:3**) said, *"Thou wilt keep him in perfect peace, whose mind is stayed on thee: because he trusteth in thee."* There is nothing more than the perfect peace of God.

Citizens of the Kingdom of God are blessed beyond measure, therefore, you must endeavor to become one, if you are yet to become, and to continue, if you are already one. The greatest accomplishment one should strive to have is the right to be a citizen of the Kingdom of God. Just as Christ said, you must *"Seek ye first the kingdom of God, and His righteousness; and all these things shall be added unto you."* (Matthew 6:33)

Chapter Reflections

The Kingdom

- _____
  _____
  _____

- _____
  _____
  _____

- _____
  _____
  _____

CHAPTER SIX
THE KINGDOM LIFE IN BELIEVERS

"Therefore, If a man be in Christ, he is a new creature: old things are passed away; behold, all things are become new."
- 2 Corinthians 5: 17

The Kingdom life is the lifestyle that describes or identifies citizens of the Kingdom. Just like every society has a unique trademark, it could be a meal, clothing, a language, a way of life, the Kingdom also has a kind of lifestyle that its citizens live. Paul made several statements that shows that the Kingdom life is unique, one of such is found in (**Galatians 2:2**) *"I am crucified with Christ nevertheless I live; yet not I, but Christ liveth in me: and* *the life I now live in the flesh I live by the faith of the Son of God, who loved me, and gave himself for me.*" If you don't live the lifestyle of the Kingdom, you cannot be recognised as a child or citizen of the Kingdom. Let's look at some crucial things about the Kingdom life of believers.

What the Citizens Look Like

> Salvation brings this citizenship status

(2 Corinthians 5: 17) said, *"Therefore, If a man be in Christ, he is a new creature: old things are passed away; behold, all things are become new."* Upon the receiving salvation, there is a transformation of a man and an award of citizenship that redefines the new believer. There is a cleansing that comes from the heart and rubs off on the external appearance, choices, and dealings of the believer. Salvation brings this citizenship status, and the citizenship status comes with a befitting lifestyle. Before we look at the core lifestyles of the citizen, we must understand why there should be a new lifestyle in the first place. A great illustration will be that of a common person in the society, who submitted himself for the electoral process, and was elected the governor of the state. The new status brings prestige and that prestige and honour comes with a lifestyle that reflects the class. He no longer treks long distances or enters public transport, he doesn't just stroll into any roadside eatery to grab lunch or dinner,

and he/she doesn't just tell tales and gist with any random person. He now has dos and don'ts that responsibility and position describes for him/her.

The same experience that happens at the transformation of a man from a common man to a politically empowered man happens in the life of a believer who is now a citizen of the Kingdom. Every citizen must live the lifestyle of the Kingdom, and must live by the rules governing the Kingdom. The lifestyle of the Kingdom can be seen in (**Galatians 5: 22- 23**) *"But the fruit of the Spirit is love, joy, peace, longsuffering, gentleness, goodness, faith, meekness, temperance: against such, there is no law"* in ***vs. 26*** *"If we live in the Spirit, let us also walk in the Spirit"* We see a clearer call to work in the above lifestyles. Let's take a look at some of those lifestyles pointed out.

! Righteousness in the Citizens

> *Righteousness is expected of a citizen*

Righteousness should be the primary nature and lifestyle of every Kingdom citizen. It is the beginning of a Kingdom blessed life. It is the access to several blessings that come as a citizen of the Kingdom. (***Matthew 6: 33***) says *"But seek ye first the Kingdom of God, and His righteousness: and all these shall be added unto you."* The question is what is righteousness? Righteousness is simply, doing the right thing, at all times, in all places, to everybody, in all situations, to the glory of God. Righteousness is expected of a citizen because that is the lifestyle of the king of the kingdom. It is also a lifestyle that glorifies His name, magnifies His majesty, and establishes His will on earth.

> *Righteousness entails doing what Christ will do in several situations.*

Every citizen of the Kingdom should live a righteous life if he/she must maintain a right standing with the king, or risk being banished from the Kingdom. The lifestyle of righteousness entails being in the Lord's will and purpose, while on earth. It grants you access to the riches in the Kingdom and makes you an heir of the father. Christ is the righteousness of God, and has made righteousness possible for everyone who comes to the Father through Him. Righteousness entails doing what Christ will do in several situations. It consists of living a life that stands for the right regardless of whose ox is gored. Righteousness is a mind-set that is based on the infallible, unchanging Word of God. You too can cultivate that mind-set today, if you seek God's grace to live a righteous life. He is more than willing to help you do His will.

! Love Is the Lifestyle

Another lifestyle of the Kingdom citizen is Love. God is love and His children must love Him in order to please Him. You cannot please someone whom you do not love. Our goal is to love like Christ. For God so loved the world that He sent His only begotten son, that whosoever believes in Him should not perish, but have everlasting life. That is a depth of love that man may never be able to offer. However, it is an example for members of the Kingdom to follow. We love our neighbours like ourselves (Leviticus 19:18). Radical love should be demonstrated more intentionally and specifically to our enemies. In (**Matthew 5: 44)**, the Lord Jesus taught *"But I say unto you, love your enemy and pray for those who persecute you."* This is the pathway to living not only a peaceful life, but also living a life that represents Heaven on Earth. Loving our enemy heap coals of fire on their head and brings them to a point of conviction on the saving grace. It makes them see the foolishness of grudges and unforgiveness, and opens their conscience to repentance.

When we look at the characteristics of love as preached in (**1 Corinthians 13: 1-13)**, we understand what it really means to love. From that passage, we understand that Love is patient. It is not rash in decision. When you love, you exercise patience and do only the needful. Love does not envy. It teaches you to celebrate people and their successes genuinely rather than being envious of their wins. Christ cautioned the disciples at various times when they acted in jealousy, He taught them that true love celebrates with those who are celebrating and mourns with those who are mourning. Love is Sacrificial. A life of love is willing to let go of pleasure and comfort for the good of someone else. The greatest spiritual gift any believer must possess is love. *"And now abideth faith, hope, charity, these three; but the greatest of these is charity (Love)."*

> When you love, you exercise patience and do only the needful.

! Peace and Unity

As citizens of the Kingdom; Peace, and Unity are a necessity and a must-have. Peace fosters unity, and when there is peace, unity is built strongly. As citizens of a Kingdom it is your responsibility to ensure that we live in peace with everyone around us. (**Hebrews 12:14**) *"Follow Peace with all men, and holiness, without which, no man shall see the Lord"* The first part of that scripture, explains the criteria to see the Lord at the end as being peaceful and Holy. Something about peace is that, it is enabled by love and the grace of God. To live peacefully, the believer must look up to the life of Christ to draw inspiration from the power of peace. In (**Matthew 5 vs. 9)**, the Bible has it that *"Blessed are the peacemakers for they shall be called the children of God."* Living in peace is a lifestyle of Kingdom citizens as grace has been given through salvation in order to live the life that reflects the Father's will.

Unity is about ensuring that oneness is maintained and togetherness is ensured. It takes a peacemaker to foster unity. We must remember the power of unity as described in (**Psalm 133: 1- 3**) *"Behold how good and how pleasant it is for brethren to dwell together in Unity! ... For there the Lord commanded the blessing, even life forevermore."* It takes unity to receive some dimension of blessings. The disciples had to gather together and prayed in unity in order to receive the Holy Ghost. Unity strengthens and gives the power of a three-fold chord that cannot be broken.

> *It takes unity to receive some dimension of blessings.*

! Joy Unspeakable

The Bible says; rejoice forevermore, and again I say rejoice. When considering the fruit of the Spirit, Joy is part of it. The Joy of a Kingdom citizen comes from a place of deep understanding that not only has his sins been forgiven, but he has also gotten access to Kingdom heritage. We must seek the Joy of the Lord for that is our strength. The joy in the Kingdom citizen affects the way he does the Master's work, it brings about cheerfulness in fulfilling the divine commission. Joy is priceless and refreshing. It energizes and refreshes our zeal. Joy makes you place Jesus first, yourself last, and others in-between. We are called to a happy life-- to a life that sees the blessing of the Kingdom and rejoices in appreciation of God's acts and abilities.

(Romans 14:17) said, *"For the kingdom of God is not meat and drink; but righteousness, and peace, and joy in the Holy Ghost."*

The joy of the believer is not supposed to be tied to anything. Citizens of the kingdom must maintain a cheerful attitude every time, regardless of what the outcome might be in **(1 Thessalonians 5: 16 -18)**, we are encouraged specifically to *"Rejoice always, pray without ceasing, give thanks in all circumstances, for this is the will of God in Christ Jesus."* The joyful heart gives thanks to God, always; and is filled with thanksgiving! Jesus came to give us new life and fill us with Joy. It is His will that we live a life of abundance; that is, a life that is fulfilling and joyful. No matter what the believer passes through, he/she must remember that *"...weeping may endure for a night, but joy comes in the morning."* (Psalm 30:5b.)

Chapter Reflections

- _____
  _____
  _____
  _____

- _____
  _____
  _____
  _____

- _____
  _____
  _____

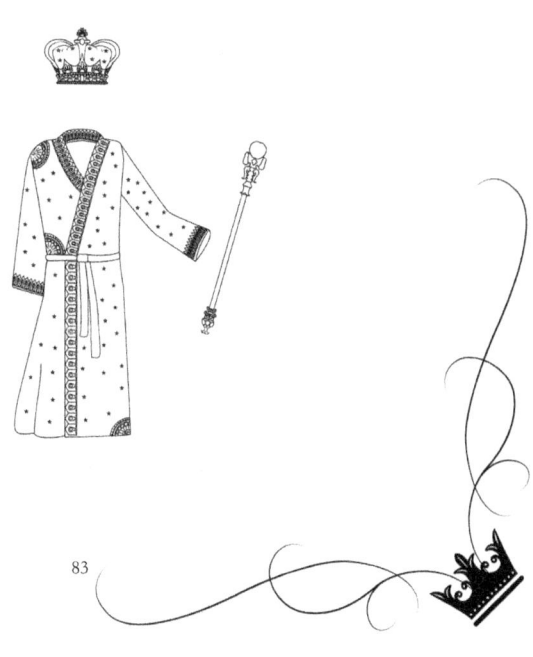

CHAPTER SEVEN
THE KINGDOM OF GOD; THE TRUE ESSENCE OF LIVING

Day after day, the things that we see and hear around, and even across the globe can be very devastating. Many people are not mentally stable, there are still cases of suicide every now and then; most people are worried, about what to eat, what to drink, and what to wear.

Matthew 6:25-33(NKJV);

"Therefore I say to you, do not worry about your life, what you will eat or what you will drink; nor about your body, what you will put on. Is not life more than food and

the body more than clothing? Look at the birds of the air, for they neither sow nor reap nor gather into barns; yet your heavenly Father feeds them. Are you not of more value than they? Which of you by worrying can add one cubit to his stature? "So why do you worry about clothing? Consider the lilies of the field, how they grow: they neither toil nor spin; and yet I say to you that even Solomon in all his glory was not arrayed like one of these. Now, if God so clothes the grass of the field, which today is, and tomorrow is thrown into the oven, will He not much more clothe you, O you of little faith? "Therefore do not worry, saying, 'What shall we eat?' or 'What shall we drink?' or 'What shall we wear?' For after all these things the Gentiles seek. For your heavenly Father knows that you need all these things. But seek first the kingdom of God and His righteousness, and all these things shall be added to you."

Jesus is speaking about the Kingdom to us, and He is saying that anyone who is burdened about the affairs of this world has not fully come into the reality of the Kingdom of God. For if we continue to worry about those things, then we are not different from the heathen whom we call unbelievers. Jesus said in *verse 33* that what we should pursue, and strive after is the Kingdom of God, for by doing so, every other thing that we need in life would be added unto us.

Earlier in the same chapter, Jesus made a very fundamental point;

"And when you pray, do not use vain repetitions as the heathen do. For they think that they will be heard for their many words."

Notice that these days; the prayers of men are filled with a lot of demands and requests. People are bothered a lot about the affairs of life that it is so evident in the way they pray. Instead of worship and praise, the prayer altar of so many folks is filled with tears of demands, reflecting their concern about the things they want to eat, drink, or wear. Instead of the Saints to intercede for the souls of men who are yet to be saved, folks go before the Lord to tender long lists of requests.

Talking about prayer, Jesus gave a model in the earlier verses of the same *Matthew chapter six;*

"In this manner, therefore, pray: our Father in heaven, hallowed be Your name. Your kingdom come. Your will be done on earth as it is in heaven. Give us this day our daily bread. And forgive us our debts, as we forgive our debtors. And do not lead us into temptation, but deliver us from the evil one. For Yours is the kingdom and the power and the glory forever. Amen. "For if you forgive men their trespasses, your heavenly Father will also forgive you. But if you do not forgive men their trespasses, neither will your Father forgive your trespasses." (Matthew 6:9-15 NKJV)

It is quite important to note carefully that the model presented above begins with worship, and the very first request that was made was that

God's Kingdom should come. If you can understand this as a believer, it will go a very long way to save you from worrying. Having this understanding will help you to know that the establishment of God's Kingdom in the hearts of men is much more important to the Father, and His intention is not just to use His people without taking care of them. God is faithful, and His integrity to keep to His Word can forever be trusted. It is, therefore, important for believers to know that the message of God's Kingdom cannot, but be preached; for that is exactly the essence of the Gospel of Jesus Christ.

The world today can be reached much more easily than ever before with the advent of various social media platforms. Although, there are many social vices on these platforms, hence, instead of getting carried away by them, we must use them as platforms to reach out to the world for Jesus. Just as the scripture has identified it as our responsibility in *Psalm 145:10-12 (NKJV);*

"All Your works shall praise You, O Lord, and Your saints shall bless You. They shall speak of the glory of Your kingdom, and talk of Your power, to make known to the sons of men His mighty acts, and the glorious majesty of His kingdom."

Even in the midst of the chaos and various challenges across the globe, we must understand that

the world cannot know peace until men come into alignment with the Kingdom of Christ; the Prince of Peace.

> *A believer must seek to please God first*

Seeking the righteousness of God simply means that one is seeking to please God. These days, we have many men who want to please others, and so sometimes, realize they sin against God. Many people are in wrong acts today, even though they do not want to be involved in those acts, but the fact that they do not understand the righteousness of God makes them choose to please men above pleasing God. A believer must seek to please God first, and not do anything that is not in alignment with God's Kingdom as a way of pleasing men. If God is not pleased, the fact that men are pleased still does not justify the act. Normally, when you stand with God, He is able to make men favour you. In other words, you become favourable by men when you seek after God's Kingdom and His Righteousness.

Luke 17:20-21 (NKJV);

Now, when He was asked by the Pharisees when the kingdom of God would come, He answered them and said, "The kingdom of God does not come with observation; nor will they say, 'See here!' or 'See there!' For indeed, the kingdom of God is within you."

Glory to God, Hallelujah! The Kingdom of God is presently present in you; it is living for that Kingdom that you derive true joy and an all-round fulfilment.

How can anyone live right in an ecosystem where the unexpected can happen at an unexpected time? One year that caught the whole world by surprise is 2020. Everyone anticipated that things would be normal, and had planned the year. Well, certain people were able to find a better way of getting things done, but all over the world, everyone was confronted by a pandemic, which reportedly took the lives of many people globally and obviously kept everyone on the lookout; as a way of being cautious and taking preventive measures.

> *How can one live in this world peacefully no matter the situation?*

Even before the pandemic, the world system was designed to come with a whole lot of anxiety, uncertainty, disappointment, failure, and everything that is not desired. Day after day, the things that we see and hear around, and even across the globe can be very devastating. Many people are not mentally stable, there are still cases of suicide every now and then; most people are worried, about what to eat, what to drink, and what to wear. The question is, how can one live in this world peacefully no matter the situation?

We are yet to explore totally a particular system of living; this system of living is yet to be adopted by everyone. This system of living ought to be the emphasis on the pulpit of every ministry. Instead, we try to adopt the world systems in a bid to find a solution to that, which our congregation is going through. The only lasting solution to whatsoever anyone might be going through is the Kingdom of God.

There is nothing as assuring as the Kingdom of God. If only everyone can adopt the Kingdom of God, even in the affairs of this world, the whole world would have been a better place. It is important for those who are already under the influence of this Kingdom to do everything in their capacity to ensure that everyone around them is aware and duly informed about this Kingdom.

> *believers must cultivate the habit of interceding for nations*

Jesus Christ, talking to His disciples in **Mathew 6**, gave a prayer model. His first emphasis was that they should not pray to God like the heathen, but rather express their petition to God behind closed doors/not to be seen. He asked them not to speak in prayer like those who believe they have to say too many things in prayer before God can understand them. In addition, while giving them a prayer model, He began by saying; "Our Father, who is in Heaven, hallowed be your name. Your

Kingdom come..." Jesus was practically proving to His disciples that we build the Kingdom of God on prayer. No one who does not understand this might be able to spread the Gospel of the Kingdom to others. Without prayer, we cannot establish the Kingdom of God in the lives of men. Instead of just asking God for what we want and need, believers must cultivate the habit of interceding for nations, that the Kingdom of God is established in them.

The Kingdom of Heaven is a real place. It is a geographical space located above the earth. That is the place where the throne of God is established, hence, beyond just sitting in Heaven, it is God's desire to sit in the heart of men. The consciousness of God in the hearts of men is the same thing as having the Kingdom of God ruling their hearts. Therefore, we can describe the Kingdom of God as God's complete sovereignty over everything that exists.

Why do we have wars, troubles, terrorism, corruption, and other social vices? It is simply because the whole world is yet to come into the knowledge of the Kingdom of the Prince of Peace. Jesus Christ is the Prince of Peace, and He wants to rule in the affairs of men. The undeniable truth is, until the whole world embraces the Lordship of Christ in all facets of life, the world will never be free from bondage and crises. It is important to know that this Kingdom of God is not a new Kingdom; it has been in existence before the whole world began.

"Therefore I say to you, do not worry about your life, what you will eat or what you will drink; nor about your body, what you will put on. Is not life more than food and the body more than clothing? Look at the birds of the air, for they neither sow nor reap nor gather into barns; yet your heavenly Father feeds them. Are you not of more value than they? Which of you by worrying can add one cubit to his stature? "So why do you worry about clothing? Consider the lilies of the field, how they grow: they neither toil nor spin; and yet I say to you that even Solomon in all his glory was not arrayed like one of these. Now, if God so clothes the grass of the field, which today is, and tomorrow is thrown into the oven, will He not much more clothe you, O you of little faith? "Therefore do not worry, saying, 'What shall we eat?' or 'What shall we drink?' or 'What shall we wear?' For after all these things the Gentiles seek. For your heavenly Father knows that you need all these things. But seek first the kingdom of God and His righteousness, and all these things shall be added to you." (Matthew 6:25-33 NKJV)

In **verses 25-33 of Mathew 6**, Jesus began to address the major fears and anxieties of men. A whole lot of things usually burden many people. Jesus said; *"Take no thought for your life."* This statement does not mean that you should not plan; it simply means that you should not worry. When your planning is overwhelmed by worry, it is not a way of life for those in God's Kingdom. In fact, the majority of the people living on the surface of the earth, if not all, planned the kind of 2020, they envisaged; but then, the unexpected happened. This is a way of proving to humanity, that our plans must be subjected to God's pattern; we cannot carelessly plan without subjecting our plans under God's absolute plan. God is not the one responsible for the evil, but He sees ahead and knows what is going to happen, which we might not know until He shows us. Showing us what is ahead, will help us in our planning, and will make us increase our dependence on Him.

Three major things Jesus identified as the worry of men are:

- What to eat

- What to drink

- What to wear

Jesus said, concerning the three things above, believers should not worry. Actually, worry does not solve the problem, it only adds to it. We live in a world where many people are so burdened about what they want to eat, drink, and wear. Repeatedly, the fashion world introduces new styles and everyone just wants to have the latest. Economists have concluded that the needs of men are insatiable.

Then, the Kingdom principle is; do not worry about those things. If you continue to worry about what to eat, drink, or wear, that you can no longer sleep, it is a very great sign of unbelief.

> Seek first the Kingdom of God.

In *verse 33*, Jesus Christ said; *"But, seek you first the Kingdom of God and His righteousness..."* Instead of worrying, Jesus is saying to every believer, "Seek you first the Kingdom of God..." Instead of you panicking, instead of allowing the things of this world to be your concern, Jesus is saying; "Seek first the Kingdom of God." Do not forget, seeking the Kingdom of God is;

- Being conscious of God in everything

- Being conscious of the sovereignty and authority of God

- Seeking to do that which pleases God in all things

- Seeking to do only that which God wants us to do

The greatest gift of God to humanity is embedded in His love. If believers would be able to seek the righteousness of God, we must do it based on the expression of God's love to the people. How best can we express that love? This is by telling them about the Kingdom of God.

We cannot talk about God's love without concrete emphasis on "Giving." One other way to show love to people is by giving to them. Every believer should cultivate the habit of giving. You can always touch a life; you can always reach out to someone; you can bless someone with your excessive substance. You do not need to have so much before being a blessing, even from that which you think is little, and God can use you to touch a life.

The operations of God's Kingdom can be best understood when we pay close attention to the study of the book of Revelations. In the **15th to 19th verse** of **Revelation 11**, the Bible reveals that every Kingdom of this world is still coming under the authority of the Kingdom of Jesus. The Kingdoms of this world can only last as long as this world exists; hence, the Kingdom of God lasts forever.

"Now when He was asked by the Pharisees when the kingdom of God would come, He answered them and said, "The kingdom of God does not come with observation; nor will they say, 'See here!' or 'See there!' For indeed, the kingdom of God is within you." (Luke 17:20-21 NKJV)

There is something powerful that Jesus revealed here, *"...For indeed, the Kingdom of God is within you."* You do not have to wait until you get to Heaven before you begin to experience the Kingdom of God. The Kingdom of God is right there inside of you. You have the mind of Christ right there inside you. You do not need to travel far to meet anyone to bring the Kingdom of God to you. Right there, inside you, there is the Kingdom of God; if truly you are a believer, the Kingdom of God is in existence within you!

Chapter Reflections

- _____
  _____
  _____

- _____
  _____
  _____

- _____
  _____
  _____

CHAPTER EIGHT
FULFILLING YOUR SPECIFIC ASSIGNMENT IN THE KINGDOM

Every believer was once a sinner. He/she belonged to the Kingdom of darkness and was under the control and influence of the flesh. Some were in a state of hopelessness; they did not know what was right to do about their lives. Some were in the wrong association, mingling with folks who had sold their soul to the devil. But then, there is a fact that cannot be changed, Jesus Christ died for the sin of the whole world, and His blood He shed for the redemption of every soul on the surface of the earth. For as many who had been privileged to accept this fact, they gain their freedom from the bondage of sin and the devil, and eventually, they become better people, who shall be useful in the hand of the Lord, God Almighty for the salvation of others. Every believer was preached to before he/she believed; a believer must, therefore, arise for the salvation of others.

> *A believer must, therefore, arise for the salvation of others.*

One thing that is important for all believers to understand is that every believer has been called out of darkness into God's Light, so that while they walk in the darkness of this world, they would be able to shine God's Light, which the darkness of this world can never comprehend. It is, therefore, necessary for every believer to understand that he or she is called out of darkness into the marvellous light of Christ.

Being called in Christ has nothing to do with holding a leadership position in the Church. Every believer has been called, and there is a specific assignment that every believer is called to do. Until we first understand that God had called us, we will not be able to pursue this responsibility. Therefore, the foundation of this exposition is laid on the basis that every believer has a calling, and that the calling is not specific to a set of believers, but universal to the community of believers. What then is this calling all about?

"Later He appeared to the eleven as they sat at the table; and He rebuked their unbelief and hardness of heart, because they did not believe those who had seen Him after He had risen. And He said to them, "Go into all the world and preach the gospel to every creature. He who believes and is baptized will be saved; but he who does not believe will be condemned. And these signs will follow those who believe: In My name, they will cast out demons; they will speak with new tongues; they will take up serpents; and if they drink anything deadly, it will by no means hurt them; they will lay hands on the sick, and they will recover." (Mark 16:14-19 NKJV)

(Mark 16:14-19) records the account of Jesus' appearance to the eleven apostles. Having rebuked them for their unbelief, He said to them in verse 15; *"Go into all the world and preach the gospel to every creature"*.

The first thing to note in that verse is the word "Go." The word "Go" There signifies a command. Jesus was not advising His disciples, neither was

He asking them for a favour. He was giving them instruction, telling them what they must do, even as He was departing from them.

> *Go ahead and invade the systems of the world*

The next thing that comes to mind is, *"Go where?"* Jesus said; *"Go into all the world..."* The *"World"* in this verse is from the Greek word; "Cosmos," and it can mean two things; System, and, nations. Jesus asked His disciples to go ahead and invade the systems of the world. Notice that He did not ask them to go start a Church, His instruction was clear and specific; *"Go into all the world..."*

Many times, people focus a lot on the pulpit ministry. Whenever it comes to fulfilling the Divine mandate, our attention is usually limited to the pulpit. We were made to believe that the Divine Mandate is limited to a particular set of people, but Jesus is saying to His disciples here, "Go and invade the systems!" What systems are we talking about here? We are talking about the Economy, Banking and Finance, Mass Media, Medicine, Pharmacy, Engineering, Education, Business, Aviation, Politics, Commerce and Industry, Sport; amongst others. Jesus said; *"Go into all the world..."* Men are needed to stand for God in all these systems, if all the men who are in those systems today are believers, the world would have become a better place. The emphasis is, men are not only needed to serve the Lord on the pulpit before a congregation, and men are needed to represent the Kingdom of God in every system of this world.

> *The Gospel can be preached effectively through the character and leadership disposition of men.*

Then, Jesus went further in the same verse to say, "...*and preach the gospel to every creature.*" Preaching the Gospel of the Kingdom is not limited to just the opening of one's mouth, the Gospel can be preached effectively through the character and leadership disposition of men. If a believer in politics represents the Kingdom of God well, the people will be convinced to believe in the power of God's Kingdom. No matter which system or nation anyone has decided to represent the Kingdom, one thing that is important to note is that the Gospel must be preached. The Gospel must be preached verbally, and be demonstrated in every system and nation.

One other fundamental point to note is that Jesus did not say; "...preach the Gospel to every man," He said; "...preach the Gospel to every creature." In other words, we can say that the word "Creature" here refers to everything that the Lord has created that is in existence. Just as the Bible says in (**Romans 8:19**); *"For the earnest expectation of the creation eagerly waits for the manifestation of the sons of God."* This simply means that, the manifestation of the Sons of God is not only being expected by men, but by everything that is in existence. The Sons of God are to fulfil their part of the prophecies.

Jesus revealed some very powerful revelations in the **17th and 18th verses of Mark 16.** Jesus said, *"And these signs shall follow those who believe: In My name, they will cast out demons; they will speak in new tongues; they will take up serpents; and if they drink anything deadly, it will by no means hurt them; they will lay hands on the sick, and they shall recover."*

Jesus is never going to send anyone to the entire world without certain signs following him or her. These signs are confirmations that these ones have His backing and that they are carrying out the assignment based on His authority. What signs did Jesus talk about in this passage?

- Casting out demons;
- Speaking in new tongues;
- Protection from any form of evil;
- Healing the sick

It is important to note that the promise of protection here does not mean the same as careless living. It does not mean that a believer can decide to hold a snake or drink anything poisonous in order to prove a point. Jesus was only saying, that peradventure, they were attacked with these things, there is a guarantee of safety, just that those who decide to attack them with such evil can surrender to the superiority of the power of God.

Moreover, while doing according to this instruction, every believer needs to understand that the message of the gospel is not the same as publicizing one's church, neither is it the same as amplifying the image or personality of a church leader, it is simply the message of God's Kingdom. If we are to preach the Kingdom, it means, we cannot do that without talking about the King of that Kingdom. The King of that Kingdom is Jesus Christ, and He must be the central figure of our message.

"I will extol You, my God, O King; And I will bless Your name forever and ever. Every day I will bless You, and I will praise Your name forever and ever. Great is the Lord, and greatly to be praised, and His greatness is unsearchable. One generation shall praise Your works to another, And shall declare Your mighty acts. I will meditate on the glorious splendor of Your majesty, And on Your wondrous works. Men shall speak of the might of Your awesome acts, And I will declare Your greatness. They shall utter the memory of Your great goodness, And shall sing of Your righteousness. The Lord is gracious and full of compassion, Slow to anger, and great in mercy. The Lord is good to all, and His tender mercies are over all His works. All Your works shall praise You, O Lord, and Your saints shall bless You. They shall speak of the glory of Your kingdom,

And talk of Your power, To make known to the sons of men His mighty acts, And the glorious majesty of His kingdom. Your kingdom is an everlasting kingdom, and Your dominion endures throughout all generations. The Lord upholds all who fall, And raises up all who are bowed down. The eyes of all look expectantly to You, And You give them their food in due season. You open Your hand And satisfy the desire of every living thing. The Lord is righteous in all His ways, Gracious in all His works. The Lord is near to all who call upon Him, To all who call upon Him in truth. He will fulfill the desire of those who fear Him; He also will hear their cry and save them. The Lord preserves all who love Him, But all the wicked He will destroy. My mouth shall speak the praise of the Lord, And all flesh shall bless His holy name Forever and ever." (Psalms 145:1 – 21 NKJV)

Psalm 145 talks a lot about the Kingdom of God. The first verse started with a revelation of praise to the King. Every King deserves to be praised, hence, in God's Kingdom, though He also deserves to be praised, He does not depend on our praise to be God; He's God all by Himself. One major point that every believer must understand is that, whatever Christ is to you now, He is forever the King. Though, Jesus Christ may be a healer to you right now, He might be a provider to you right now, He might be the oil of gladness to you right now, He might be anything you think He is to you right now; He has an eternal role in God's

Kingdom, and that is what He would be forever - King.

In the ***10th - 13th verse of Psalm 145***, the Psalmist continues with a much more, deeper revelation about the description of God's Kingdom. Specifically, in ***verse 11***; the Psalmist says; *"They (His saints) shall speak of the glory of Your Kingdom, and talk of Your power."* The Bible did not say that, "All the pastors shall speak of your Kingdom..." It's not the title that determines the role; it is only determined by the status of any individual with God. If you are a believer, you have the mandate to proclaim the message of God's Kingdom. The ***13th verse*** of the same chapter reveals the duration of God's Kingdom. The Kingdom of God is forever, and not a seasonal kind of government that only exists for a while. No king on earth reigns forever. If an earthly king does not die, he can be dethroned. Hallelujah! Praise God! The Kingdom of God lasts forever; His Kingdom is from everlasting to everlasting. He is not just a king for a particular generation, He's King throughout every generation that had existed and the ones that will still exist. In addition, after the earth has passed away, His Kingdom remains the same. He cannot be dethroned; He's King forever.

The same account in *Mark 16* is recorded in the account of ***Mathew, the 28th chapter. Jesus said in verse 18***; *"...All authority has been given to Me in*

Heaven on earth". Having said that, Jesus pronounced the great commission, *"Go therefore and make disciples of nations..."* We can say, that Jesus was basically saying to His disciples, "I have the authority in Heaven and on Earth, and so, on the strength of my authority, go and make disciples of nations..." No man goes on an assignment without being sent; else, he might not have a covering or backup from any higher authority. Jesus is saying to His disciples here, and by extension, every believer, that as they go to nations, they have His backing, and His authority will definitely go with them.

> *Give one's self to study, so that the Holy Spirit can teach one.*

In the *20th verse*, Jesus made a crucial statement, *"Teaching them to observe all things that I have commanded you..."* How can a man who had not been taught rise to teach others? However, being taught in this context does not necessarily mean to be under the tutelage of any formal teacher or minister alone, but to give one's self to study, so that the Holy Spirit can teach one. In order to teach the nations accurately and effectively, one must have also been a good student of the Holy Spirit.

In (***Mathew 24:14***), Jesus speaking to His disciples said, *"And this gospel will be preached in all the world as a witness to all nations, and then the end shall come."* Notice that Jesus was so sure of the fact that the Gospel would be preached in the entire world. Well, not everyone in the world may believe it, but no one would be able to deny the fact that he or she heard about it. With the advent of the social media in this present age, likely, a place can be reached without leaving one's home. That a person does not have the chance to travel abroad is no longer an excuse for not preaching the Gospel, as it is possible to travel around the whole world without leaving one's room; using the internet. Jesus said in that *14th verse* that until the gospel has reached the whole world, the end should not come. In fact, it is an undeniable fact that the second coming of Christ is closer than ever before; the end is not as far as it used to be.

Jesus, our dear Lord, and Savior, was speaking in (**Luke 4:43**), He said, *"I must preach the kingdom of God to the other cities also, because for this purpose I have been sent."* The same thing applies to every believer, we have not been saved so that we can boast about our salvation and condemn others, and rather, we were saved so that we can reach out to others, and bring them into the knowledge of the Gospel of God's Kingdom. Just as Christ was sent to the world to save it, He has also sent us to spread the message of His Kingdom across all the nations of the earth.

> *There is equity in the Kingdom of God.*

One thing that must be emphasized in our message is

that the Kingdom of God is different from the Kingdom of this world. In the Kingdom of this world, there is a whole lot of segregation; certain people can see themselves as more important than some other categories. There is a whole lot of discrimination amongst the people; contrarily, there is equity in the Kingdom of God. No one proves to be superior to the other because everyone is important to God. Jesus said in (***John 18: 36)***, "My Kingdom is not of this world..."

Jesus gave His disciples instructions in **Mathew 10 and Mark 6** about what they should expect as they go out to preach the Gospel of the Kingdom. He revealed to them that they might face many persecutions, and even be hated by many, but in all, He is with everyone that has chosen to follow Him and represent Him no matter what comes their way. Of course, following Jesus can cost a believer some things, well, if not everything. Then, no matter what a believer goes through, a believer knows that his name is written in the Book of Life, and he shall reign with Christ. Friends may leave you alone, but Jesus is a friend that will never walk away. The family may choose to despise and desert a follower of Christ, but Jesus is never going to leave His own.

In *Luke 10*, Jesus sent out the 70- disciples to preach the Gospel; He sent them out two by two. In the second verse, Jesus said; *"The harvest is tru-*

ly great, but the laborers are few..." God is not asking us to give our lives to save others; Jesus had already done that. God is asking us to go into an already prepared harvest, and win souls into His Kingdom. Jesus Christ had done the most important part of the assignment on the cross; our own role is just to tell the world that Jesus Christ died that they may eternally live.

FULFILLING YOUR SPECIFIC ASSIGNMENT IN THE KINGDOM

Chapter Reflections

- _____
  _____
  _____
  _____

- _____
  _____
  _____
  _____

- _____
  _____
  _____
  _____

CHAPTER NINE
KINGDOM REPRESENTATIVES

Elijah as a representative of God's Kingdom

People are giving up on the Word of God, and the second coming of the Lord is imminent. The Bible says, "The love of many shall wax cold." At such a time as this, we need the Word of God for us to represent God as expected. Elijah represented the King of kings and the living God. Elijah is a man of God. The prophets of Baal serve many gods, but Elijah serves one God. The prophets of Baal together with the people served gods with no eyes to see, ears to hear or mouth to speak.

> *"Then Elijah said, "As the Lord of hosts lives, before whom I stand, I will surely present myself to him today." So Obadiah went to meet Ahab, and told him; and Ahab went to meet Elijah. Then it happened, when Ahab saw Elijah, which Ahab said to him, "Is that you, O troubler of Israel?" And he answered, "I have not troubled Israel, but you and your father's house have, in that you have forsaken the commandments of the Lord and have followed the Baals. Now therefore, send and gather all Israel to me on Mount Carmel, the four hundred and fifty prophets of Baal, and the four hundred prophets of Asherah, who eat at Jezebel's table."* (1 Kings 18:15-19 NKJV)

Elijah told King Ahab that he and his father's house have forsaken the commandments of the Lord and followed false gods. Then, he asked him to gather all the prophets of Baal together at Mount Carmel. He began to address the issues of indecision in their hearts. The Bible says,

> *"So Ahab sent for all the children of Israel, and gathered the prophets together on Mount Carmel. And Elijah came to all the people, and said, "How long will you falter between two opinions? If the Lord is God, follow Him; but if Baal, follow him." But the people answered him not a word. Then Elijah said to the people, "I alone am left a prophet of the Lord; but Baal's prophets are four hundred and fifty men."* (1 Kings 18:20-22 NKJV)

Many times, people are indecisive, and this makes them falter between two opinions. They do not know who or what to follow. They do not know who or what to believe. They are confused and full of doubt and anxiety. Elijah had to address the people of whom they believe and what they believe. The situation that surrounded them had made them shift grounds. They lost the gaze of God and got their hearts and eyes fixed on idols.

Elijah challenged them that if the Lord is God, they should follow Him. If the Lord is God, follow Him, and if Baal, follow him. There is no point in serving two masters. Out of the prophets in the land, Elijah stood for God; he did not care if he was the only one. There are times that our decision to serve God will make us stand-alone. Until we learn to stand alone, we might not stand out for God. The way of God is not a popular path taken by many; only a few finds it.

"Therefore let them give us two bulls, and let them choose one bull for themselves, cut it in pieces, and lay it on the wood, but put no fire under it, and I will prepare the other bull, and lay it on the wood, but put no fire under it. Then you call on the name of your gods, and I will call on the name of the Lord; and the God who answers by fire, He is God." So all the people answered and said, "It is well spoken." Now Elijah said to the prophets of Baal, "Choose one bull for yourselves and prepare it first, for you are many;

and call on the name of your god, but put no fire under it." (1 Kings 18:23-25 NKJV)

Then, Elijah created a challenge. He asked them to call upon their gods. He was so confident in the God he served. The prophets of Baal agreed to the challenge.

"So, they took the bull which was given them, and they prepared it, and called on the name of Baal from morning even till noon, saying, "O Baal, hear us!" But there was no voice; no one answered. Then they leaped about the altar which they had made. And so it was, at noon, that Elijah mocked them and said, "Cry aloud, for he is a god; either he is meditating, or he is busy, or he is on a journey, or perhaps he is sleeping and must be awakened." So they cried aloud, and cut themselves, as was their custom, with knives and lances, until the blood gushed out on them. And when midday was past, they prophesied until the time of the offering of the evening sacrifice. But there was no voice; no one answered, no one paid attention." (1 Kings 18:26-29 NKJV)

Elijah made a mockery of their God by asking the prophets of Baal whether the god was sleeping or went on vacation. The people that worship the living God will always boast in the power of God. They do not glory in their weaknesses but in the strength of God. They do not glory in their power but in the power of God.

Elijah wanted to show that the God he was serving is the true and living God. He wanted them to see the true and living God in action. Sometimes, people do not believe because they cannot see results, and it is our responsibility to bring down God's power in our business, home, and organizations through excellence and integrity.

"Then Elijah said to all the people, "Come near to me." So all the people came near to him. And he repaired the altar of the Lord that was broken down. And Elijah took twelve stones, according to the number of the tribes of the sons of Jacob, to whom the word of the Lord had come, saying, "Israel shall be your name." Then, with the stones he built an altar in the name of the Lord; and he made a trench around the altar large enough to hold two seahs of seed. And he put the wood in order, cut the bull in pieces, and laid it on the wood, and said, "Fill four waterpots with water, and pour it on the burnt sacrifice and on the wood." Then he said, "Do it a second time," and they did it a second time; and he said, "Do it a third time," and they did it a third time. So the water ran all around the altar, and he also filled the trench with water." (1 Kings 18: 30 - 35 NKJV)

Elijah understood the protocol for hosting God. He set the altar in order and arranged it in such a way that followed the ancient patterns. The first thing he did was to repair the altar. Then, he took twelve stones that represent the number of tribes of Israel and the covenant name of Israel.

"And it came to pass, at the time of the offering of the evening sacrifice, that Elijah the prophet came near and said, "Lord God of Abraham, Isaac, and Israel, let it be known this day that You are God in Israel and I am Your servant, and that I have done all these things at Your word. Hear me, O Lord, hear me, that these people may know that You are the Lord God, and that You have turned their hearts back to You again." Then the fire of the Lord fell and consumed the burnt sacrifice, and the wood and the stones and the dust, and it licked up the water that was in the trench. Now when all the people saw it, they fell on their faces; and they said, "The Lord, He is God! The Lord, He is God!" (1 Kings 18:36-39 NKJV)

> God desires to manifest His power and glory in our lives and through our lives

Elijah said, "Let it be done according to your word." When it comes to demonstrating God's power, it is about fulfilling God's Word and not our selfish desires. It is about establishing God's will, and not our will. God desires to manifest His power and glory in our lives and through our lives; the challenge is our readiness to do His will.

When God gives His people divine instructions, He also gives strategies to overcome the enemy. If we desire God's kind of results, we need to obey God's divine instructions. Elijah did according to the Word of God. God does not want us to be confused, so He gives us His word to guide us through our steps on earth.

> *Your victory is sure in Christ.*

We can see that the other prophets of Baal do not have the supernatural power that Elijah had. What a mighty God we serve! When God has given us victory, all we need to do is to keep standing. Your victory is sure in Christ. He secures your success. Your victory glorifies the Father.

The enemies you see today, you shall see them no more, and that is the power of God. When God gives you the head of your enemy, you will be able to face the giants. Elijah stood for God and demonstrated to the people that God is Lord. God will fight for you, and make people see that He is Lord is your life.

Hezekiah, a Representative of God

"In those days Hezekiah was sick and near death. And Isaiah the prophet, the son of Amoz, went to him and said to him, "Thus says the Lord: 'Set your house in order, for you shall die, and not live.'" Then he turned his face toward the wall, and prayed to the Lord, saying, "Remember now, O Lord, I pray, how I have walked before You in truth

and with a loyal heart, and have done what was good in Your sight." And Hezekiah wept bitterly. And it happened, before Isaiah had gone out into the middle court, that the word of the Lord came to him, saying, "Return and tell Hezekiah the leader of My people, 'Thus says the Lord, the God of David your father: "I have heard your prayer, I have seen your tears; surely I will heal you. On the third day, you shall go up to the house of the Lord. And I will add to your days fifteen years. I will deliver you and this city from the hand of the king of Assyria, and I will defend this city for My own sake, and for the sake of My servant David." Then Isaiah said, "Take a lump of figs." So they took and laid it on the boil, and he recovered. And Hezekiah said to Isaiah, "What is the sign that the Lord will heal me, and that I shall go up to the house of the Lord the third day?" Then Isaiah said, "This is the sign to you from the Lord, that the Lord will do the thing which He has spoken: shall the shadow go forward ten degrees or go backward ten degrees?" And Hezekiah answered, "It is an easy thing for the shadow to go down ten degrees; no, but let the shadow go backward ten degrees." So Isaiah the prophet cried out to the Lord, and He brought the shadow ten degrees backward, by which it had gone down on the sundial of Ahaz." (2 Kings 20:1-11 NKJV)

Hezekiah was sick and close to death. The prophet told Hezekiah that he was going to die. This must have been heart-breaking news for him. Hezekiah did not engage the prophet in the discussion. He did not start to lament. Rather, he turned to God.

The Bible says, *"Then he turned his face toward the wall, and prayed to the Lord, saying, 'Remember now, O Lord, I pray, how I have walked before You in truth and with a loyal heart, and have done what was good in Your sight."*

Whom do you turn to when you are in difficult situations? When it seems that there is no way forward, where do you turn to? Hezekiah turned to the wall and face God. The wall signifies an end. He knew that God could bring a new beginning to a seemingly ending thing. He knew that there are matters that are beyond the power and influence of a man that only God can settle.

When your life pleases God, He will please you. God answered the prayer of Hezekiah. He is the God that can save your soul; your defender when others give up on you; your present help in the time of trouble. Let God fight your battles. Some battles are beyond your power. These battles are not for you to fight. This is why God tells you that He will fight for you and you shall hold your peace ***(Exodus 14:14 NKJV)***. To win every battle, cover yourself with the blood of Jesus Christ.

There will be trials and temptations, but you must be willing to allow God to fight for you. We can learn a great deal from the letter of James. It says,

"My brethren, count it all joy when you fall into various trials, knowing that the testing of your

faith produces patience. But let patience have its perfect work, that you may be perfect and complete, lacking nothing. If any of you lacks wisdom, let him ask of God, who gives to all liberally and without reproach, and it will be given to him. But let him ask in faith, with no doubting, for he who doubts is like a wave of the sea driven and tossed by the wind. For let, not that man suppose that he will receive anything from the Lord; he is a double-minded man, unstable in all his ways." (James 1:2-8 NKJV)

The Amplified version adds beauty to it. It reads:

"Consider it wholly joyful, my brethren, whenever you are enveloped in or encounter trials of any sort or fall into various temptations. Be assured and understand that the trial and proving of your faith bring out endurance and steadfastness and patience. But let endurance and steadfastness and patience have full play and do a thorough work, so that you may be [people] perfectly and fully developed [with no defects], lacking in nothing. If any of you is deficient in wisdom, let him ask of the giving God [Who gives] to everyone liberally and ungrudgingly, without reproaching or fault-finding, and it will be given him. Only it must be in faith that he asks with no wavering (no hesitating, no doubting). For the one who wavers (hesitates, doubts) is like the billowing surge out at sea that is blown hither and thith-

er and tossed by the wind. *For truly, let not such a person imagine that he will receive anything [he asks for] from the Lord, [For being as he is] a man of two minds (hesitating, dubious, irresolute), [he is] unstable and unreliable and uncertain about everything [he thinks, feels, decides]"* (James 1:2-8 Amplified Bible).

You need wisdom to go through difficult times. God says, "If you lack wisdom, ask." Wisdom is necessary to go through trials and temptations. Wisdom makes you allow God to fight your battles. When things turn out well, people might say you are wise. They did not know that true wisdom is allowing God to fight on your behalf.

> *God is good.*

There was a day I was meditating, and my mind went to the Good Samaritan. A man was robbed, injured, and left in pain by the roadside. The Good Samaritan came and helped him. God is good. When you find yourself in helpless situations, God will send you an angel. When you are by the roadside, He will attend to your worries. The Bible says,

"Fight the good fight of faith, lay hold on eternal life, to which, you were also called and have confessed the good confession in the presence of many witnesses." (1 Timothy 6:12 NKJV)

When we entertain strangers; you very well so entertain angels. Do not give up on God and never doubt the power of God. When you are tired of fighting, call on God and He will strengthen you. Sometimes, you do not have faith, build your faith by putting your trust in His word.

God require much from us because to whom much is given, much is required. When you are at a crossroads, and you feel like giving up, remind yourself that you are not just on earth on your own accord; you are on earth because God wants you here. Remind yourself that you are fighting the good fight of faith. God is depending on you. Irrespective of what you are going through, never forget that God has called you for a purpose. The Bible says,

"And we know that all things work together for good to those who love God, to those who are called according to His purpose. For whom He foreknew, He also predestined to be conformed to the image of His Son, that He might be the firstborn among many brethren. Moreover whom He predestined, these He also called; whom He called, these He also justified; and whom He justified, and these He also glorified." (Romans 8:28-30 NKJV)

He called you to be justified. He justified you to be glorified. Do not give up because God is at work. The Bible says,

"Behold, I am the LORD, the God of all flesh: is there anything too hard for me?" (Jeremiah 32:27 KJV)

There is nothing too hard for God to do. God is depending on us to fulfil the great commission by standing for Him and representing Him in every area of our lives.

KINGDOM REPRESENTATIVES

Chapter Reflections

- _____
  _____
  _____

- _____
  _____
  _____

- _____
  _____
  _____

CHAPTER TEN
KINGDOM GENERALS

Life is different things to different people. To some people, life is a race, and everyone is in the race like athletes, running towards a finish line. While some see life as a race, some other folks see it as a game, where it is either you win or lose depending on how smart you are. Actually, a closer look at life will definitely prove to one that life is warfare, and that battle is the clash of two Kingdoms.

There used to be a worshipper in God's Kingdom, who was revered more than most of the Angels in God's Courtyard, if not all. He had access to the

Throne-Room and was always there worshipping the Creator of all things that are in existence. With his level of access to God, he thought he knew all that he needed to know, in order to become a god. This general in God's army forgot that the life he was living was not his own, he must have forgotten that he is equally a creature and had not been given the mandate to become the creator. His quest to be in-charge got him charged for rebellion, and he was kicked out of God's presence, just because he wanted the image of God.

> *Creation of man birthed jealousy*

Eventually, God introduced another dimension of Himself by creating a being in His image and after His very own likeness **(Genesis 1:27),** which He called MAN. This creation of man birthed jealousy, and Lucifer, the general that fell from his original position with an everlasting judgement hanging over him, became so curious about doing something to mankind that will make a man lose his position as the image of God.

His quest began with the first man, as he manipulated the serpent and used him as access to influence Eve, the first woman that ever lived. Eve fell for the deception, and Adam, the man himself, fell for love, and could not resist his wife's proposal. They ate the fruit that God had told them not to eat, and thereafter, the unimaginable happened.

Their eyes were opened, they were naked, and felt so disconnected from the life of God.

While declaring judgement over the serpent, God made a prophetic statement;

"So, the Lord God said to the serpent: "Because you have done this, you are cursed more than all cattle, and more than every beast of the field; on your belly you shall go, and you shall eat dust all the days of your life. And I will put enmity between you and the woman, and between your seed and her Seed; He shall bruise your head, and you shall bruise His heel." (Genesis 3:14-15 NKJV)

Pay closer attention to **verse 15**,

"And I will put enmity between you and the woman, and between your seed and her Seed; He shall bruise your head, and you shall bruise His heel."

> *The enemy is only attacking the image that kicked him out.*

There is a war, and you and I were born into it. This war had been going on for eternity, and until the end of time, this war will not end. The truth is, it is not all about you being attacked, the enemy is only attacking the image that kicked him out. When humanity fell out of the plan of God in the Garden of Eden, the enemy thought it was over and that he had won. Glory to God, there was another plan. God Himself came to the earth as a man, to redeem humanity from the curse that disobedience brought on them, through Jesus Christ.

(John 3:16);

"*For God so loved the world that He gave His only begotten Son, that whosoever believes in Him shall not perish, but have everlasting life*".

(2 Corinthians 5:17);

"*Therefore, if any man is in Christ, he is a new creation, old things have passed away; behold, all things have become new.*"

Glory to God, if you are a believer, your victory is secured in Christ Jesus; you are only claiming the battle that Christ had already won. Hallelujah!

However, what should a believer do after understanding that he has victory in Jesus' name? Should a believer fold his arms, waiting for the roll call in Heaven? One thing a believer must not forget is that, if nobody had preached to him, he would have remained in bondage, and there are millions of souls out there in the same bondage who would never be free if nobody preached to them. The battle remains with the clash of Kingdoms; the devil really wants to have many people on his side as he anticipates his eternal judgement.

Revelation 12:1-17(NKJV);

"Now a great sign appeared in heaven: a woman clothed with the sun, with the moon under her feet, and on her head a garland of twelve stars. Then being with child, she cried out in labor and in pain to give birth. And another sign appeared in heaven: behold, a great, fiery red dragon having seven heads and ten horns, and seven diadems on his heads. His tail drew a third of the stars of heaven and threw them to the earth. And the dragon stood before the woman who was ready to give birth, to devour her Child as soon as it was born. She bore a male Child who was to rule all nations with a rod of iron. And her Child was caught up to God and His throne. Then the woman fled into the wilderness, where she has a place prepared by God that they should feed her there one thousand two hundred and sixty days. And war broke out in heaven: Michael and his angels fought with the dragon; and the dragon and his angels fought, but they did not prevail, nor was a place found for them in heaven any longer. So the great dragon was cast out, that serpent of old, called the Devil and Satan, who deceives the whole world; he was cast to the earth, and his angels were cast out with him. Then I heard a loud voice saying in heaven, "Now salvation, and strength, and the kingdom of our God, and the power of His Christ have come, for the accuser of our brethren, who accused them before our God day and night, has been cast down. And they overcame him by the blood of the Lamb and by the word of their testimony, and they did not love their lives to the death. Therefore rejoice, O heavens, and you who dwell in

them! Woe to the inhabitants of the earth and the sea! For the devil has come down to you, having great wrath, because he knows that he has a short time." Now, when the dragon saw that he had been cast to the earth, he persecuted the woman who gave birth to the male Child. But the woman was given two wings of a great eagle, that she might fly into the wilderness to her place, where she is nourished for a time and times and half a time, from the presence of the serpent. So the serpent spewed water out of his mouth like a flood after the woman, that he might cause her to be carried away by the flood. But the earth helped the woman, and the earth opened its mouth and swallowed up the flood which the dragon had spewed out of his mouth. And the dragon was enraged with the woman, and he went to make war with the rest of her offspring, who keep the commandments of God and have the testimony of Jesus Christ."

You being a believer alone, the battle is against your soul, and it will take some measure of discipline to remain focused. A believer must be able to balance his walk with God with the consciousness of the ongoing warfare, in order to live with the mentality of a soldier of Christ.

Generals in the military are aware as soon as they join the military as soldiers that they can die at any time during military action. A General knows fully well that he cannot run away from death, while he places his soldiers on the war-front, hence, he leads the other soldiers to the battlefield as they aim for victory over their enemies. Knowing fully well that they are obligated to their nation, generals (soldiers) see themselves as properties of their nation; as they are owned by the state and can be sent to military action anytime any day.

Before now, God had been raising many Generals. From generation to generation, God continued to raise men who were leading other men into the battle and were following His Divine order. One of them is Joshua.

Joshua 1:9 (NKJV);

"Have I not commanded you? Be strong and of good courage; do not be afraid, nor be dismayed, for the Lord your God is with you wherever you go."

Joshua 1:14-18;

"Remember the word which Moses the servant of the Lord commanded you, saying, 'The Lord your God is giving you rest and is giving you this land.' Your wives, your little ones, and your livestock shall remain in the land which Moses gave you on this side of the Jordan. But you shall pass before your brethren armed, all your mighty men of valor, and help them, until the Lord has given your brethren rest, as He gave you, and they also have taken possession of the land which the Lord your God is giving them. Then you shall return to the land of your possession and enjoy it, which Moses the Lord's servant gave you on this side of the Jordan toward the sunrise." So they answered Joshua, saying, "All that you command us we will do, and

wherever you send us we will go. Just as we heeded Moses in all things, so we will heed you. Only the Lord your God be with you, as He was with Moses. Whoever rebels against your command and does not heed your words, in all that you command him, shall be put to death. Only be strong and of good courage."

The scripture above is an account of Joshua's ordination into the leadership of Israel, and the commencement of his leadership assignment. He was more of a warrior, as he led Israel out of the wilderness into the Promised Land after the death of Moses. There are a few things to draw from this account:

1. There is a Land to Conquer

None of us can say that everyone in the land we currently occupy has come to the knowledge of the Gospel of Christ. There is a land to conquer; there is a land to win for Christ.

What most believers do today is complain about what certain unbelievers are doing and the reckless life they are living, without any compassion directed to soul winning. Nobody is saved by the complaints of others; everyone that was saved was saved because the seed of the Gospel was planted in the field of their heart. Actually, there is nothing the Holy Spirit will work on in the heart of men, if no seed was planted in them, in the first place. Therefore, as Kingdom Generals, we have to be conscious of our assignment in order to take the land for Jesus. Until every sinner around us comes to the knowledge of Christ, we cannot stop working.

> Be conscious of our assignment

One of the painful things in the ministry today is how Kingdom Generals are distracted by selfish pursuit, and the church of Christ is seen as a business centre where ministers are taking advantage of their members to make money. As a Kingdom General, you possess authority when it comes to winning souls, as you cannot just sit in church and expect men to come; you will have to go to them as Jesus had commanded in the Great Commission. You cannot stay in the backyard and tell people to come, you have to go to the street and claim lost men to the Kingdom of God.

Mediocrity is not supposed to be the life of a Kingdom General, as Power and Influence are major tools in reaching out to souls. God is not just looking for men who can speak, as the Kingdom of God is not just all about speaking; it is a Kingdom of Power *(1 Corinthian 4:20)*. Kingdom Generals must not settle for less, as God expects us to represent Him in every sphere of life.

In order to be effective in this war-front, there is armour that we need to put on;

Ephesians 6:10-20 (NKJV);

"Finally, my brethren, be strong in the Lord and in the power of His might. Put on the whole armor of God that you may be able to stand against the wiles of the devil. For we do not wrestle against flesh and blood, but against principalities, against powers, against the rulers of the darkness of this age, against spiritual hosts of wickedness in the heavenly places. Therefore take up the whole armor of God, that you may be able to withstand in the evil day, and having done all, to stand. Stand therefore, having girded your waist with truth, having put on the breastplate of righteousness, and having shod your feet with the preparation of the gospel of peace; above all, taking the shield of faith with which you will be able to quench all the fiery darts of the wicked one. And take the helmet of salvation, and the sword of the Spirit, which is the word of God; praying always with all prayer and supplication in the Spirit, being watchful to this end with all perseverance and supplication for all the saints— and for me, that utterance may be given to me, that I may open my mouth boldly to make known the mystery of the gospel, for which I am an ambassador in chains; that in it I may speak boldly, as I ought to speak.

2. Ask God for Abundant Peace

When God gives you abundant peace, you become much more effective in your service to the Lord. Even in the midst of the battle of life, personally, you need peace to be able to "Fight with soundness and much more confidence."

Moreover, the following points are also noteworthy as Kingdom Generals;

- They fight for each other, no one competes with the other; we are in the same army.

- Use every available means to reach the world for Jesus, as long as it can reach men, you never can tell the soul that will be saved through such a medium.

- You cannot die before your time, no matter how tough the battle seems to be in your region.

- In the military system, a General must have won many battles; a Kingdom General is also supposed to have won many souls for Jesus.

Chapter Reflections

- _____
  _____
  _____
  _____

- _____
  _____
  _____
  _____

- _____
  _____
  _____
  _____

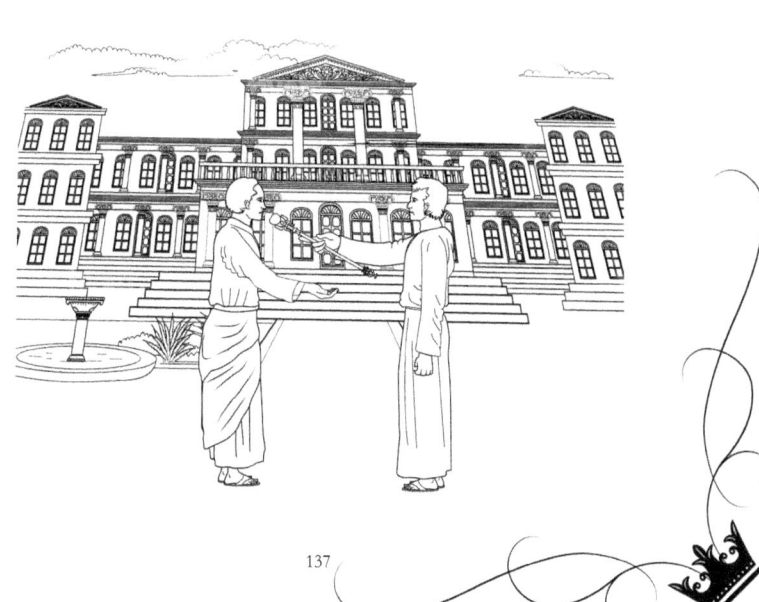

CHAPTER ELEVEN
THE EMERGENCE OF NEW KINGDOM LEADERS

He was trained to know the law, a Pharisee and a persecutor of everyone who believed Christ. He was there when the first martyr was stoned to death; in fact, he was the one looking after the garments of those who stoned him. He had successfully received the approval from the High Priest and those in authority in order to imprison believers and have them eventually killed. All this, he was doing with the mind of fighting for God, and kicking against a new faith, which was seen as a deviation from the dictates of the law.

Eventually, the Lord broke His silence, and interrupted his journey to Damascus. He was converted himself, and began to preach the same Gospel that he had kicked against.

With all that he did against the Church, Paul the Apostle, formerly known as Saul of Tarsus, gave a powerful revelation in Romans chapter eight:

> *For the law of the Spirit of life in Christ Jesus has made me free*

"There is therefore now no condemnation to those who are in Christ Jesus, who do not walk according to the flesh, but according to the Spirit. For the law of the Spirit of life in Christ Jesus has made me free from the law of sin and death." (Romans 8:1-2 NKJV).

The moment you give your life to Christ, there is no more condemnation to you. It does not matter what you have done in the past or how you lived your life. It has nothing to do with your past because you have a new beginning in Christ, and you are a new creature. Look at how Paul confidently spoke in the above scripture. One would not have expected that Saul of Tarsus would ever be qualified to call upon God, talk less of being referred to as an Apostle of Jesus Christ. However, with the revelation of who he is now in Christ, He says; *"There is therefore no more condemnation..."* It does not matter who you used to be, an encounter with Jesus would definitely turn your life around for good. You cannot meet Jesus and your life remains the same! If you had truly met Jesus, your life must be known to have changed.

> *You cannot meet Jesus and your life remains the same!*

As much as I celebrate the achievement of Paul the Apostle, my major concern is that, if one man named Paul could go round the world preaching, why can fifty of us not do more? How about a thousand of us? How about ten thousand of us? There are churches everywhere; hence, hanging around activities is not all that is required from us as leaders. It is God's desire that the whole world be saved; and until that has happened, we cannot just be folding our arms.

The issue that most folks have is that because of what they had done in the past, they feel not worthy enough; and that is exactly what the enemy intends to achieve. He wants to cripple your Kingdom mind-set, and make you feel unqualified to share your salvation experience. However, just as Paul shared in the above scripture, you must believe that you have no past records, as far as God is concerned. You have no more condemnation; you are worthy in Christ.

A closer look at a few more verses in the same Romans chapter eight;

"So then, those who are in the flesh cannot please God. But you are not in the flesh, but in the Spirit, if indeed the Spirit of God dwells in you. Now if anyone does not have the Spirit of Christ, he is not His. And if Christ is in you, the body is dead because of sin, but the Spirit is life because of righteousness. For as many as are led by the Spirit of God, these are sons of God."

There are two major points we can draw out from the above scripture;

1. You Are Dead To the Flesh

Being dead in the context of the scripture above does not mean that you are not alive; it only means that you no longer have the ability to respond to whatsoever you are dead to in the flesh. There are a whole lot of fleshly things out there that engross people. Drugs, drunkenness, sexual immorality, amongst many others are the things that many people struggle with today; hence, anyone in Christ is dead to these things. This simply means, he no longer has feelings/desires for such anymore.

There is a whole lot of stuff on the internet today, and a whole of people are being distracted every now and then. However, instead of being distracted by those media platforms, we can go ahead and use them to spread the message of the Kingdom of God, with the aim of reaching out to a global community for the sake of The Kingdom.

2. You Are Alive To the Spirit

To be alive to the Spirit simply means that the Spirit of God leads you. Moreover, if the Spirit of God leads you, you are the Son of God. It is important to know that "Son-ship" in this context has nothing to do with gender or age; instead, it is all about Spiritual Maturity. The Bible says,

"For as many as are led by the Spirit of God, these are sons of God" (Romans 8:14 NKJV)

One of the meanings we can derive from the word "Son" is "Child." Moreover, when a person is someone else's child, he or she is the representation of that individual. Being the child of God simply means that you are the image and likeness of God. One thing that everyone should know is that there is the image of God in every human. If truly we know this, we would stop viewing people from the perspective of their color and that demonic strategy called "Racism," and even "Sexism," will end. You must see your neighbor as a carrier of God's image and likeness, and that is what will make you respect them. You do not respect men because of who they are or where they are from, you only do that with the understanding that every human is the image and likeness of God.

One word that can be substituted for "Image" in this context is "Nature." Therefore, we can say that there is the nature of God in every human.

One factor that validates the nature of God in every believer is the presence of the Holy Ghost in us, and with the Holy Ghost at work in us, we are limitless.

The same Holy Ghost was at work in Jesus Christ during His earthly ministry. They saw His physical realities, but did not understand the spiritual plan. They did not know that Jesus Christ was not going to end it on the cross, and that there was a higher plan than that. They could only torture His body, but His spirit was alive, working on the path of victory for humanity. He caught death and the Kingdom of darkness by surprise and gave victory to us.

It is in that victory that you have your confidence as a Kingdom Leader. You have what it takes to lead; you have what it takes to spread the Gospel to nations. You cannot continue to allow your gender, experience, or status to limit you. If truly you are born again, you must rise for the salvation of others.

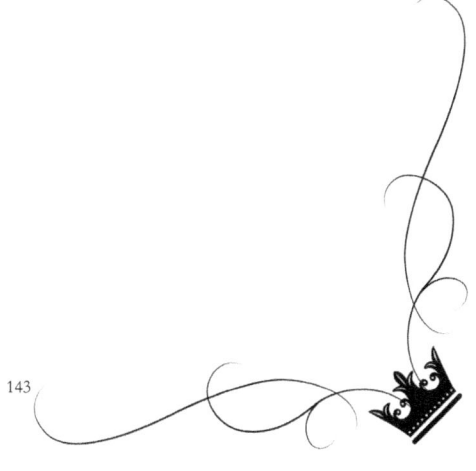

Chapter Reflections

- _____
  _____
  _____

- _____
  _____
  _____

- _____
  _____
  _____

CHAPTER TWELVE
UNDERSTANDING SONS & SONSHIP

Romans 8:14 *"For as many as are led the Son of God."*

"The Kingdom of God doesn't come with outward appearance. It manifests itself through the life of Christ that is manifested in His people." (Sons and Sonship- Hancliff)

Luke 17:21 *"Neither shall they say, Lo here! Or lo there! For, behold, the kingdom of God is within you."*

The Spirit of Christ is a person of government and authority. The Father is calling out administrators and governors for His Kingdom. He is calling out people who can take the responsibility of establishing His Kingdom; ruling and reigning with Him. Sonship allows for building the Kingdom of God through their lives. We have been called of God to Sonship to service and partnership with the Father.

The word *'teknon'* from the Greek translates "one born" and denotes immaturity. It is never used of Christ when He is spoken of as the Son of God. **Romans 8:16** *"The Spirit itself beareth witness with our Spirit, that we are the children of God."*

There is a different Greek word used above for 'sons.' The Greek word is 'Huios' and translated into English, it means descendant or offspring. It denotes maturity or one full grown.

The word is translated from the Greek word "huiothesia" and it means "the placing of a son," the placing of one who has walked in the relationship of childhood into a position of responsibility as a mature son. **Galatians 4:5** *"That we might receive the adoption of sons."*

It is God's mind to bring about the change that takes place when a child is recognized as an adult. A child, who takes the responsibilities of a Son, is able to take on the responsibility of Kingdom building. Adoption speaks of position and not relationship.

God is aiming for a relationship of gradual responsibilities. He wants us to be workers together with Him, to take on a full partnership in the business of His kingdom government.

Individuals become Sons of God by believing and by submission to the Holy Spirit. All that is required is belief in the sincere mandate of the Father. We become Sons by obedience to the Spirit.

God has a purpose for son

The Father will use obedient sons to fulfil His purpose in the earth. He will establish the Kingdom in the earth through the strategic, networking ministry of those who have entered into matured Sonship. He will use the sons to deliver the whole creation from the bondage of corruption.

Jesus had such an intimacy with God the Father. It was one of complete submission agreement and communions he demonstrated to us. The power of agreement is very strong; "How can the two walk unless they agree?" Jesus was committed to conducting the affairs of His father.

His daily life was surrounded; and consumed the Father's will and purpose. He was sensitive to represent the Father's interests at all times. He learnt obedience through sufferings. Jesus' main objective was to promote and establish the Kingdom of

God. He wanted God's rule of government and praises on the earth. Jesus spent quality time in the presence of God to hear the direction and instruction from Him. He also went into His presence to receive strength. In God's presence there is fullness of Joy.

The Father's plans for Sons

> *Only quality time asking the Father and fellowshipping with Him will true purpose be discovered.*

What are the affairs of the Father? Firstly, the Father designed a specific role and assignment for each individual to fulfil. Another human can recognize giftedness or talent blossoming. However, only quality time asking the Father and fellowshipping with Him will true purpose be discovered. Consider any relationship, one would recognize that only with spending quality time together would be the dreams of those persons and their emotions are understood. Most importantly, both parties involved begin to learn the very essence and character of the other individual. In many wonderful moments even one's own character is discovered. One would discover personal weakness and strengths and would have to make various changes in one's own character to relate in the relationship involved.

This analogy is exactly how our Father longs for a loving relationship with his children. Daddy wants us to tell Him when we hurt, and what makes us upset. He wants for us to share our vision and goals with Him. He wants to fulfil them for us. He desires to mentor and developed our lives into the beautiful thought out plans He has for our lives. Papa wants to share our most intimate moments of broken secrets; things in our lives that no one else knows. He wants to heal those shameful events of our hidden past. Father wants to heal our guilty, unbearable, shameful past. He longs to gently settle our shaky minds and revive our identity in Him.

The Father desires to share His <u>dreams, passions and emotions</u> with His Sons. Similar to any loving father, daddy wants to express what grieves Him. He excitedly waits to tell and show His children the precious gifts He has waiting. How about sitting as He speaks His plans for His family? Lastly, He wants to safely cradle us in His arm and delicately pour His assurance that we His Sons and His prized possession.

The Father yearns for the restoration of His Sons. This word son from the original language and text has two words. One word is 'Tekna', which connotes a young child, in reference to scripture; it suggests that all of humanity is the offspring or creation of God. However, the second term of 'Huios' refers to a mature son.

The Father perfects Sons

Jehovah God is the Father of all creation and sustainer of all that exists. His nature as Father is seen with His intimacy with man-Adam. The body of Christ is at a time of great movement of the Spirit. God is pouring out new insights and revelation about His word as He equips and prefect the church, His bride, to meet Him.

One of the last battles of the Spirit, will be to perfect the Christian believer. This word 'perfect' does mean that every believer will be whole or complete in all areas of their lives. This maturing process has been the heart of the Father God for many generations as He slowly revealed His nature to mankind throughout history. This is observed especially with the Hebrew people and now the church of Jesus Christ.

God is bound by His word and covenant to re-establish His relationship with mankind after Adam fell in the Garden of Eden. He is concerned with fellowship with His prized creation humans. God is seeking to restore the relationship of Father-ship to mankind. Adam had an intimate relation-ship with the Father among great levels of relation of God and man, creator and creative being. It was a Father-Son relationship.

God as a father had a heart like any earthly father to bear an offspring, a seed that would continue the His affairs. Similarly, as earthly fathers desire a seed that resembles them and would continue the name and the genetics or the seed of the father. Hence God desire to conform man truly after His image and likeness. These words suggest a number of qualities and characteristics of God and hence man. "God is a Spirit and they that worship Him must worship Him in spirit and in truth."

Hebrews 12:5 *"And you have forgotten that of encouragement that addresses you as sons: My son, do not make light of the Lord's discipline and do not lose heart when He rebukes you,"*

(vs. 6) *"Because the Lord disciplines those He loves, and punishes everyone He accepts as a Son."*

Hence, mankind is the very genetic seed of God. Man is the gene of God, unlike the other creatures that were made by the very thought of God. God proposed to make man with His very hand to breathe or place His very nature into man ('Pneuma' – 'breathe of Spirit'). Adam had a relationship with God among levels of relations of God and man, creator and creative being. He had a Father – Son relationship. On the other hand, one of the messiah's enthronement names is "Eternal Father" *"And His name shall be called Wonderful, Counsellor, The mighty God, the Everlasting Father, and the Prince of Peace."* **(Isaiah 9:6)**

Many today are in search of true identity. This is one of the greater problems in our world. This world is filled with people who lack an understanding of who they are. Many are searching aimlessly in all areas, including education, career, finances and relationships to occupy the void in their lives. The true identity of the born again Christian believer comes from knowing where they come from or in other terms that their Father is. Understanding who we are is pivotal in foreseeing where we are going. Who we are tells us our strengths in various areas of our lives and also our weakness. It gauges our self -confidence and measures our potential. It determines our comfort in developing meaningful relationships with others.

Fatherhood is a strong form of self-regulation for developing a person's character development. Naturally, a father in the home provides a young girl with security, self – perception and a model of good men in her life. Likewise, a young man forms his early perception of maleness and identity of manhood from his father.

The whole family is cantered on the order of father. Similarly, in the spiritual realm, our heavenly Father wants to import destiny, direction and daily development into the lives of His children. This special interest in His creation is not always received by many but is acquired through Sonship. This is a covenant relationship inherited through

Jesus Christ and sealed by God's Spirit verifying that we are His children.

Romans 8:14 *"For as many as are by the Spirit of God, they are the sons of God."* **(vs. 15)** *"The Spirit itself beareth witness with our spirit, that we are the children of God."*

Jesus, the first Son became the one through whom came many Sons of the Father. Through sonship we learn the inheritance God has delegated to His sons. We understand the Royal family line that runs through our veins. We are a part of a kingly family; the children of a King.

Romans 8:9 *"But ye are not in the flesh, but in the Spirit if so be that the Spirit of God dwells in you. Now if any man has not the Spirit of Christ, he is none of His."* **(vs. 14)** *"For as many as are led by the Spirit of God, they are the sons of God.* **(vs. 15)** *"For ye have not received the Spirit of bondage again to fear; but ye have received the Spirit of adoption, whereby we cry Abba Father."* **(vs. 16)** *"The Spirit itself beareth witness with our spirit, that we are the children of God :(* **vs. 17)** *"And if children, them heirs; heirs of God and joint – heirs with Christ." If so be that we suffer with Him, that we may be also glorified together."*

Paul the writer of Romans, explosively reveals the power of the believer in Jesus Christ. Paul summarizes the nature of every human's potential to become a son of God. He expresses the life of the Spirit. Spiritual sonship is the life led by the 'paraceletos', the Holy Spirit. Sonship is a life submitted to the direction of the Holy Spirit. The heavenly Father yearned to establish His continuous stream of fellowship and love when He created His son Adam in the book of Genesis. Adam was to represent the expressed nature, character and authority of the Heavenly Father on earth as the Father ruled in Heaven.

Adam was to propagate the spiritual righteous DNA of the Father throughout the ages: - human offspring. Mankind was to rule the gardens, the animals and the earth realm and be co-heir the spiritual realm with the Father. Adam was to expand the kingdom ruler-ship of the Father in the earth with complete obedience and harmony with daddy.

All of Adam's offspring was to rule in harmony and righteous order and alignment with the natural commands of the Father. Adam represented the spiritual sons of God and the gene was to continue in power; protected from the destructive elements of sin and the environment.

The book of beginnings, Genesis, expresses the disconnected relationship of Adam, the son with the Father. Adam dishonoured the relationship with the Father and lost the benefits of being a Son of a King. Adam lost fellowship through the

Holy Spirit's presence that gave him supernatural power, wisdom, creativity, council and streams of God-like abilities. Most importantly, Adam's 'God – like' genes were mutated and now He operated in a lower level of function. It made it impossible to continue the seed or DNA of God in purity to humanity throughout the generations. Adam lost abilities to govern the affairs of the earth in order to the Father's heart. He was disconnected with the purposes of the Father's mind; and the vision of the Father through Adam was clouded.

The glorious agenda of Kingdom conquest and partnership ruler-ship with man in the earth seemed threatened and impossible. The enemies of the Kingdom agenda of the Heavenly Father mocked and chuckled to the demise of the Father's dream. It seemed as if the Father's business was about to hit bankruptcy. He was going to lose all of His shares over the earth. The son had rebelliously given the power of attorney to a corrupt fired employee, the devil. Satan, the devil was now the major shareholder over the earth by technicality and severed man from his creator.

Through manipulation in the Garden, Satan legally acquired the power of attorney and ownership over the earth. He also got lease to every human that would be produced by Adam. All men therefore were born is sin and shaped in iniquity; and the seed or DNA of Satan was injected into the genetic architect of man. Satan had clones to expand his diabolical seed to the earth through the sons of God.

For thousands of years the Kingdom of God suffered violent attacks. The restoration of a race that would revive the genetics of the Father suffered tremendous distortion. The scriptures account the patriarch Abraham, as being the forerunner of God's agenda to reclaim the seed and re-estab-lish His sons in the earth.

The spiritual climate was overcast with wickedness in the earth for hundreds of years. Immorality, disorder and rebellion to the commands of the Father were prevalent.

Humanity had drifted furlongs away from the original vision of the father's empire. Man now dimly mirrored the nature, character, love and righteous ruler-ship of their heavenly Father. The Father was so disgusted that He grieved and was sorrowful that He ever created man. Mankind became, outside children, bastards who had no God-like identity. In fact, they had taken a new identity and resembled the rebellious, distorted, corrupted, adopted step-father Satan. Mankind, from the fall of Adam now worked in the family business of Satan, as co-heirs and executive directors in the Kingdom of Darkness.

The scriptures give vivid accounts of the heavenly Father's passive and patient plead for humanities fellowship. Yet through His plea and tremendous promises, mankind through the children of Abraham rejected Him. He continuously forgave and protected the children of Israel during their progression in life. The Father had found a people to begin the restorative process of re-establishing sons in the earth. His awesome presence in man was banded from communication with him. His holy presence was key to the 'Zoë' life of His sons. The 'Zoe' life is the 'God-life' that was in the order and righteous-ness of the Father. 'Zoe' life was the life of the Holy Spirit in which the identity of being a Son of God was important on the minds of every son. The 'Zoe' life in the Holy Spirit was the existence where the laws of the Father were imbedded in the minds of the Sons.

The Parakletos, the comforter, and advisor would intimately direct the sons into truth and righteousness. 'Paracletos', the Holy Spirit would unleash in every obedient son rivers of insights wisdom, revelation of the father's nature.

The Holy Spirit in the sons would empower them to walk in great authority on behalf of the Father over every situation and circumstance. The Spirit filled son would be protected from disease and death and hence walk daily in the 'Shalom' of the Father.

Sons would experience the 'shalom', meaning the **'completeness, wholeness and prosperity'** in every area of their lives. This was the Father's delight to celebrate in the wealth and shalom of His sons.

The descendants of Abraham were eyed by the Father to restore His plan of Co-ownership with mankind in the earth.

However, there was a barrier to the fulfilment of maturation of children of Sons through the Parakletos. The nations lacked the indwelling and resting upon by the presence of the Holy Spirit. Mankind was repulsive to the saturation of the Father's Holy presence and the training of man was delayed. The Father had a brilliant plan to conquer this minor dilemma. He established the King's tutoring services. This service was to govern and prepare the children underage spiritually to matured sons. This was until the moment when access would be granted in the earth for the indwelling tutor of the Holy Spirit. The Holy Spirit would then continue and complete the maturation of the spirit and mind of the sons to the heart vision and purpose of the Father. The Holy Spirit would empower the sons to overcome and destroy the contaminated gene of Satan in their flesh nature. He would train the lost sons on how to whip the desires of self, sin, and bring them subject to the laws and order of the Father Holy nature.

Paracletos, the Holy Spirit would equip and activate the sons, in their own unique way to build relentlessly the Kingdom of the Father in the earth. The sons would be consumed with the reclaiming of all spheres for the Father's sovereign rulership.

> The Holy Spirit would equip and activate the sons

Galatians 4:1-9

(vs. 1) *"Now I say, that the heir as long as he is a child, differeth nothing from a servant though he be lord of all;*

(vs. 2) *"But is under tutors and governors until the time appointed of the father.*

(vs. 3) *"Even so we, when we were children; were in bondage under the elements of the world:*

(vs. 4) *"But when the fullness of the time was come, God sent forth His Son, made of a woman, made under the law,*

(vs. 5) *"To redeem them that was under the law, that we might receive the adoption of sons.*

(vs. 6) *"And because ye are sons, God hath sent forth the Spirit of his son unto your hearts, crying, Abba, Father.*

(vs. 7) *"Wherefore thou art no more a servant but a son; and if a son; then an heir to God through Christ."*

(vs. 8) *"Howbeit then, when ye knew not God, ye did service unto them which by nature are no gods.*

(vs. 9) *But now, after that ye have known God, or rather are known of God, how turn ye again to the weak and beggarly elements, whereunto ye desire again to be in bondage?*

Paul in the book of Galatians magnificently summarizes the order and restoration of the sons of God. Built with every person is the potential to become a Son of God and heir to the Kingdom of the Heavenly Father. All humanity outside of the obedience and adoption of the heavenly father is an heir identity. Hence an heir outside of the relationship and knowledge of their inheritance is no greater than a servant.

> *Built with every person is the potential to become a Son of God*

For example, a child of an owner of a food franchise chain. That child has access to all of his father's business, resources and influences. However, the father in an effort to mature the son hires him as a janitor in one of the restaurants. The son enjoys the experience and salary he makes but is ordered by his supervisors daily to do manual task. That son is learning responsibility and experiencing maturity as he climbs that ladder of success to now become a cashier. Sadly, his father dies and leaves the entire franchise with over one hundred stores to the son. However, disturbingly the son is unaware that he has been left the franchise in a will and continues to work as a cashier.

This son is ignorant of his true identity as the father's heir to all his assets. He is blinded to his new position of authority and ownership. In parallel, many persons live in the same disposition with the heavenly father in the earth.

Millions of humans have the inheritance of the earth and the indwelling presence of the Holy Spirit's resource. But they are unaware of it. Many prefer to work tiredly as a servant and not take authority as the delegated owners of all the heavenly Father has for them in the earth.

Humanity struggles with the identity as being lords of all but instead settles for being servants. Similarly, scenarios throughout scripture are in current times. Humanity has been in the restricted halls of the University of Life. Religion and religious activity now forms the world' philosophy and cage the lost Sons of God operation. Rituals and spiritual activities institutionalize the bastard sons until they receive the liberty that is in Jesus Christ.

> *Jesus came to mend the gap between the father and the wayward sons*

It is through the only begotten Son Jesus Christ, that access is granted directly to fellowship with the Father's portfolio. Jesus came to mend the gap between the father and the wayward sons of the earth. Jesus came to restore the kingdom life in the mentality of the sons. Thoroughly, Jesus took His own blood and DNA and shed it so that mankind can have access to the Father's restored nature.

Jesus came to restore the lineage of spiritual sons and daughters in the earth. He became the perfect prototype of the Father's nature, love, essence, character, authority and order in the earth once again. Mankind now had a model of the Father's express image in the earth. Jesus came to call many sons back to the Father. The lease of Satan's reign over the earth and strangle hold on the image of God's fallen son is over.

The key that held the sons in bondage and shackle was taken by the Son Jesus. He transacted an act of sacrifice of His life. He through legal rights and humanly partnership crafted a plan and executed restoration of fellowship of man and the Father through the Holy Spirit.

Jesus reintroduces the Kingdom of the Father is was recruiting volunteers of sons into partnership for conquest in the earth. He demonstrated His power over disease, the environment, nature and sin. Jesus spoke harshly to disease and told them to leaves the bodies of 'lost sons'. He rebuked the wind and waves. He walked on water; told a fig tree to dry up and it did.

He walked victoriously reprogrammed the DNA of sin implanted in man through rebellion in the Garden of Eden. Jesus triumphed over the nature of Satan and violently resisted any nature to partner with Satan to establish the devil's Kingdom.

He overcame and dispelled demons out of operating in the realm of this earth. Jesus' accounts clearly indicated that He was about re-establishing the business of the kingdom in the earth. His Father's business was about to be revived out of collapse. A new manager and CEO were in town and plans of restoration of the Father affairs were imminent. He requested the Father to restore Him to His former state of glorious power; authority, and wealth after His death on the cross.

Previously, Jesus requested from the owner that the advisor who was with Him always be given to the new sons that He has chosen for the Kingdom cooperation. The Parakletos would stay with them, upon them and even in them, forever to accelerate the maturation process. The advisor is the person of the Holy Spirit would continue to remind the sons of the nature and purpose of Jesus lead them to all that is truthfully and convict them of rebellion to the nature of the Father.

The Holy Spirit would also by legal transfer adopt new sons and process them into true sons who would walk in great inheritance.

Galatians 4:5 *"To redeem them that were under the law, that we might receive the <u>adoption of sons</u>.* **(vs. 6)** *"Because ye are sons, God hath sent forth the Spirit of His Son into your hearts, crying, Abba Father.*

(vs. 7) *"Wherefore thou art no more a servant, but a son; and if a son, then an heir of God through Christ."*

Spiritual sonship is not a concept limited to sex or gender but of identity in the heavenly Father through Jesus Christ. For the scriptural text sons represent male and female, boy and girl, young and old, including all nationalities that accept Jesus Christ as the Saviour.

Spiritual sonship represents the disposition of mankind to the submission, obedience and direction of the Holy Spirit's voice. Sons are the matured believer who has grown from the lifestyle of sin and who walks in the nature, image and power of Jesus.

Spiritual sonship produces power to **reign** and to **exercise** authority. The Bible says, *"But as many as received Him, to them gave He power to become the sons of God."*

Power is the ability to get results. Therefore, the mark indicating whether or not one walks in spiritual sonship is one's your ability to get positive results. Achieving your place of spiritual sonship means: "Spiritual sons are defined as men and women who by the power of God brings deliverance and liberty to mankind. Spiritual sons disarm forces of wickedness and bring the creature out of the bondage of corruption into the glorious liberty of the son of God. Spiritual sons are those who through an understanding of their divine nature act like God on the earth. Sons are those who understand their divine nature." (Apostle Emmanuella Mchatton- "The Turning Point").

Romans 8:19 *"For the whole creation (all nature) waits expectantly and longs earnestly for God's – not God's son, but for God's sons to be made known (waits for the revealing, the disclosing g of their sonship."*

To be a son of God means that you recognize the nature of God residing within you. That realization will move you above the natural, through the power of the Holy Spirit, to the realm of the supernatural.

The seed potential of Sonship is on the inside of every person who's born into this earth.

Galatians 4:1-2 says: *"Now I say, that the heir, as long as he is a child, differeth nothing from a servant, though he be lord of all; "But is under tutors and governors until the time appointed of the Father."*

Authentic spiritual sonship requires righteousness, earnest prayer, integrity and knowing the authority of Jesus' name. Jesus' name releases the

anointing the electric current that flows and gives power in the lives of His children.

Sonship Scriptures:

I John 3:9 *"No one who is born of God Will continue to sin, because God's seed remain in him; he cannot go on sinning, because he has been born of God. This is how we know who the children of God are and who the children of the devil are; anyone who does not do what is right is not a child of God; nor is anyone who does not love His brother."*

Romans 8:14 *"For as many as are led by the Spirit of God, they are the sons of God."*

(vs. 15) *"For ye have not received the spirit of bondage again to fear; but ye have received the Spirit of adoption, whereby we cry Abba Father."*

(vs. 16) *"The Spirit itself beareth witness with our spirit that we're the children of God."*

The Father's plan as defined by the book of Genesis was to establish His kingdom into the earth realm. He in His infinite wisdom crafted the earth and heavens.

He strategically planted a wonderful garden for His precious son, Adam. He formed man in His own image and likeness to express His **character, nature, love** and **kingly** authority in the earth.

The nature of the Father was vividly express as God, source, protection, and King. Each of His characteristic features portrays a nature that mankind can unlock and operate in while living in the earth. Each individual possess the capacity- built into their spiritual gene to reproduce the nature of the Father in the earth.

The heavenly Father as God has a desire like any earthly papa to produce offspring, or seed to continue the affairs of His kind. The Father desired a seed that resembles Him and would continue the name and genetics of the father. Hence from the book of Genesis the heavenly Father made mankind in the very genetics of God. Man is the DNA of God, unlike the other creatures that were made by the very thought of God. There is no mention that the colourful peacock, flamboyant flamingo or ferocious lion were made in the image and likeness of the Father.

Jehovah God is the progenitor and Father of all creation and sustainer of all that exists. His nature as Father has been expressed with His intimacy with man – Adam and creation. Adam had a relationship with God among levels of relation of God. He demonstrated the protocol of a Father-Son relationship in His pre-fallen state.

In the book of beginnings, the Father is seen talking directly to Adam. The Father gave him all the resources need to be successful in the order and righteousness of the Father. The Father walked and fellowshipped with Adam in the cool of the day. The relationship was strongly intact.

The Father longs for complete fellowship with every human being. We have the tremendous opportunity to be reunited with our God, Father and friend, Hallelujah!!!

Chapter Principles

- The Spirit of Christ is a person of government and authority.

- The Father is calling out administrators and governors for His Kingdom.

- He is calling out people who can take the responsibility of establishing His Kingdom; ruling and reigning with Him.

- The Father's plan as defined by the book of Genesis was to establish His kingdom into the earth realm

- Mankind is the very genetic seed of God. Man is the gene of God, unlike the other creatures that were made by the very thought of God.

- Jehovah God is the progenitor and Father of all creation and sustainer of all that exists. His nature as Father has been expressed with His intimacy with man – Adam and creation

- Authentic spiritual sonship requires righteousness, earnest prayer, integrity and knowing the authority of Jesus' name.

- Jesus reintroduces the kingdom of the Father is was recruiting volunteers of sons into partnership for conquest in the earth.

Chapter Reflections

- _____
  _____
  _____
  _____

- _____
  _____
  _____
  _____

- _____
  _____
  _____

CHAPTER THIRTEEN
THE CHURCH AND THE KINGDOM

"Teaching them to observe all things whatsoever I have commanded you: and, lo, I am with you always, even unto the end of the world. Amen." – Matthew 28:20

The word Church is from the Greek word ekklēsia. In the New Testament, it refers to the entire body of believing Christians all over the world (Matthew 16:18), it also, is used for the believers in a particular area (Acts 5:11), and of the congregation meeting in a particular house— for example, the "House-Church" (Romans 16:5).

The Church is the body of Christ, established to prepare the saints to live as pilgrims on earth, while getting ready for the coming of Christ, to take the church home into His kingdom.

The Church is not just about the building, it's neither the Cathedral nor the Dioceses. It's not the beautiful altar, excellently aligned pews, or well-decorated interior. The Church is about the people living in it.

The relationship between the Church and the kingdom of God is best categorized into 2.

The Church helps to mould believers into living a Kingdom life while on earth. The Church exposes the believer to Kingdom principles that have been revealed and understanding how to grow in the will of God. It also, prepares the believer for the life hereafter. First, the future Kingdom; where we will reign with Christ forever, and ever.

The place of the Church in preparing citizens for the Kingdom cannot be overemphasized. Let's see some key things about the Church and the Kingdom of God.

The Responsibility of the Church to the Kingdom.

The Church was instituted after the death of Christ with the purpose of carrying out the last commission Christ gave to his followers. (**Mark 16.15**) *"And he said unto them, Go ye into all the world,* *and preach the gospel to every creature."* The purpose of Christ's birth was to save the lost through His death. During His 33-years on earth, He charted the course for the salvation of humankind. In 33-years, He started and completed the core of His mission – Salvation. On rounding up, there were many more lives to be reached and channelled to the final sacrifice that He has made, hence the great commission.

> *It is the will of the Father that many are saved*

While Christ was undergoing His earthly mission, He reached out to souls with His disciples. At some points, He sent them out in twos. **(Luke 10:1)** *"After these things the Lord appointed other seventy also, and sent them two and two before His face into every city and place, whither He Himself would come."* The aim of those movements was to win souls, to draw souls unto Him. It is the will of the Father that many are saved, and if this salvation that has been brought will reach the lost, then, someone must take it to them, and help others grow in it.

After the cross, the disciples gathered together to execute this commission as a group we know as "The Church."

The responsibility of the church includes;

a.) To preach the saving grace about Christ crucifixion. The Church being a body of saved sinners have a responsibility of reaching out to others in order to accept the salvation they have found. We were saved to save others. If our salvation was all we needed to be alive for, then we should have died after finding and embracing the cross. But, the commandment to every believer is, "Go and preach the gospel in every land."

b.) To enlarge the kingdom. The Church has a responsibility to contend with forces of darkness that seeks to prevail against it. Though our *weapons of warfare are not carnal*, we (as the church) have a responsibility to engage in this warfare on our knees. The fight is to ensure the preservation of the saints, to pull down strongholds in families that act as a stumbling block to Kingdom enlargement, to war against the devil's plans, and seek the face of God to thwart such wicked enterprise. The Church needs to grow the Kingdom by praying.

> *The fight is to ensure the preservation of the saints*

c.) To build a community of Heaven bound Kingdom citizens, that labour together in faith, till the day of the Lord Jesus. The Bible makes it clear that iron sharpens iron – and this is what the church does with its members in preparation for the Kingdom.

Of all the many responsibilities of the church towards the Kingdom of God, the most significant is the great commission – preaching of the Gospel.

In other to achieve this, the Lord Jesus promised the Holy Spirit to the disciples, and the founding members of the church. ***(Acts.1:8)*** – "But ye shall receive power, after the Holy Ghost is come upon you: and ye shall be witnesses unto me both in Jerusalem, and in all Judaea, and in Samaria, and unto the uttermost part of the earth." This promise was fulfilled when the Church gathered together to pray in (***Acts 2:1-4)*** said, "*And when the day of Pentecost was fully come, they were all with one accord in one place. And suddenly there came a sound from heaven as of a rushing mighty wind, and it filled all the house where they were sitting. And there appeared unto them cloven tongues like as of fire, and it sat upon each of them. And they were all filled with the Holy Ghost, and began to speak with other tongues, as the Spirit gave them utterance."* The effect of this was felt in the preceding chapters as the church grew and multiplied, and souls were saved daily.

Preaching the Kingdom Message

The message that attracts people to the Kingdom, and brings them in to stay, and remain is the GOSPEL. Believers are called to preach the Gospel, as it is the world that it saves. It is the Kingdom Message. In (***Matthew 24:14)***, Jesus said, "*And this gospel of the kingdom shall be preached* *in all the world for a witness unto all nations; and then shall the end come."*

The Kingdom message;

- Edifies the soul
- Renews the mind.
- Convicts the sinner.
- Offers hope of salvation.
- Points to the cross for redemption.
- Breaks the hardened hearts to accept Christ.

Any message that is not the Gospel, will only pamper people's propensity to sin. Just like the Disciples and Apostles didn't preach themselves. In **(2 Corinthians 4: 5)**, the Apostle Paul said, *"For we preach not ourselves, but Christ Jesus the Lord; and ourselves your servants for Jesus' sake."* We must ensure that we preach Christ and Him crucified. We see in **(Acts 8:5)** that *"...Philip went down to the city of Samaria, and preached Christ unto them."* We also read this testimonial about the early Church in **(Acts 5: 42)** that, *"And daily in the temple, and in every house, they ceased not to teach and preach Jesus Christ."*

We live in an age where ministers focus on the benefits of the Kingdom more than the message that attracts people into the Kingdom. At best, what such message will produce is a crop of religious people with head knowledge at best, and no heart transformation. That is not the ministry Christian leaders have been called to do. We must preach the message that glorifies God and prepares citizens for the Kingdom of God.

Preparing Everyone for the Future Kingdom

As we have earlier seen, part of the responsibility of the Church is to prepare the saints for Heaven, to get the citizens ready for the Kingdom, which God has promised.

There is a Heaven to gain. There is a Kingdom to inhabit. See *(John.14:2, 3)* *"In my Father's house are many mansions: if it were not so, I would have told you. I go to prepare a place for you. And if I go and prepare a place for you, I will come again, and receive you unto myself; that where I am, there ye may be also."*

A family needed to go on an annual vacation to Fiji Island. This year, there was something different from the previous years; there was a 9- months old baby. It was no longer going to be business as usual, where they just pick a knapsack, pack their luggage, and runoff, joining to buy whatsoever they forgot. They needed to take ample time to be sure that everything needed, more importantly, for the baby was well catered for. The scrupulous mother took days to prepare for the journey, and had no issues throughout the vacation.

Beloved believers in Christ, the future Kingdom we look forward to, demand our preparation to ensure we get there. There will be rough and tough times. There will be moments when all you need is encouraging words, or a word of prayers. We must get ourselves ready first, as individuals who make up the Church, and as a Church collectively.

The Church should prepare believers for the kingdom through;

- Establishing of regular fellowship time among the brethren- (***Psalm 133: 1-3***).

- Praying for one another and admonishing one another.

- Meeting the needs of the needy amongst us, as this strengthens their faith in God, than giving up.

- Reaching out to the sinners in our neighbourhood with the Word of God.

There is never a time to be lax about our faith. The devil is determined to see that he doesn't let anyone make it to the Kingdom of God. He was once there, and has lost his place such that he can never regain it; hence, he is desperate in his fight against our entering. Believers must remember what Christ said in (***Matthew 11:12)***, which said that "*And from the days of John the Baptist until now the kingdom of Heaven suffers violence, and the violent take* *it by force."* The force needed to comes from the cross and a sustained relationship with the king.

There are two kingdoms – The Kingdom of darkness, and the Kingdom of God. (***Matthew 7:13, 14***) said, *"Enter ye in at the strait gate: for wide is the gate, and broad is the way, that leadeth to destruction, and many there be which go in there at: Because strait is the gate, and narrow is the way, which leadeth unto life, and few there be that find it."*

Chose you this day, which kingdom you'll be a citizen of. May the Lord give you the grace to be a citizen of the Kingdom of God in Jesus' name? Amen.

The Kingdom

Chapter Reflections

- _____
  _____
  _____

- _____
  _____
  _____

- _____
  _____
  _____

CHAPTER FOURTEEN
THE FUTURE KINGDOM

"And I saw a new heaven and a new earth: for the first heaven and the first earth were passed away; and there was no more sea." – Revelation 21:1

The initial plan of God for a Kingdom where He and man will rule was changed at the fall of man. Man, the glory of His creation lost the community that was meant to give him eternal life, but a plan of redemption was made and it rescued man.

Assurance of a Future Kingdom

> *Behold I go to prepare a place for you.*

There is a future Kingdom for everyone who believes in the name of the Lord. This Kingdom has been made available as promised by our Lord, Jesus Christ, when He said; "Behold I go to prepare a place for you." For believers to have access to this Kingdom, they must go through the cross, the cross brings about our acceptance as citizens in the Kingdom, but to have the full manifestation of living in the Kingdom as promised by our Lord Jesus Christ we, therefore, look for that blessed hope that is in Christ Jesus. Jesus said in **(John 14:2, 3)** *"In my Father's house are many mansions: if it were not so, I would have told you. I go to prepare a place for you. And if I go and prepare a place for you, I will come again, and receive you unto myself; that where I am, there ye may be also."* That is the hope of believers and that is the hope of those who died in Christ. There are a lot of misconceptions about the Kingdom of God and the future Kingdom that has been promised to Believers. Some people believe that in salvation, we are already living in the Kingdom Christ promised and that there is no other Kingdom to inherit, or to look forward to. This is inconsistent with the promise of our Lord, Jesus Christ. In the Book of Revelation, we, the believers are made to understand that there would be a marriage supper of the lamb after the rapture, which will usher us into Heaven, while the great tribulation occurs. After this, will be the second coming of the Lord, for the millennial reign, and for the great white throne judgement where Christ will rule, reign, and judge the world. After that judgement, the believers will reign eternally with Him in the new Heavens and a new Earth. This is the Kingdom that we look forward to, it is that hope of the believer who dies in Christ.

> *Christ will rule, reign, and judge the world.*

What the Future Kingdom Looks Like

> *A place prepared for the purged.*

In the book of Revelation, we see the Apostle John describe the Kingdom of Heaven in various ways. Primarily, you need to know that it's a place of rest from the toils of this world. It is a place of righteousness, peace and joy. It is the habitation of the uncreated creator. It's a place of Holiness and only the Holy can habit it. Sin cannot dwell there, you can see (**1 Corinthians 6:9, 10)**, which said, *"Know ye not that the unrighteous shall not inherit the kingdom of God? Be not deceived: neither fornicators, nor idolaters, nor adulterers, nor effeminate, nor abusers of themselves with mankind, nor thieves, nor covetous, nor drunkards, nor revilers, nor extortionist, shall inherit the kingdom of God."* It's a place prepared for the purged. It's a place where the righteous will sing the praises of God forever and ever.

The future Kingdom is being described in several ways by the Lord Jesus Christ. (***Mark 4:30-34)***, *"And he said, whereunto shall we liken the kingdom of God? Or with what comparison shall we compare it? It is like a grain of mustard seed, which, when it is sown in the earth, is less than all the seeds that be in the earth: But when it is sown, it groweth up, and becometh greater than all herbs, and shooteth out great branches; so that the fowls of the air may lodge under the shadow of it."*

Why You Must Be In The Future Kingdom

Christ died that we may live. The purpose of His death includes rescuing us from the Kingdom of darkness into His light that our eternal life may be spent with Him. A rejection of the salvation brought through the cross is an acceptance into being a full time citizen of the Kingdom of darkness. This comes with hell fire and eternal damnation as its reward. If you would want your life to count in eternity, then you must accept Christ as your Lord and personal Saviour. The devil is a ruthless destroyer who seeks to ensure that you have no joy in eternity. He has placed several hooks and traps to get you into perpetual destruction, and the question is, would you let him succeed. That is what guarantees your being a citizen of the Kingdom of God and enjoying the blessings that comes from the Kingdom of God. Here are two core reasons why you must strive to enter into the future Kingdom prepared for you.

1. It was made with you in mind. Remember what Christ said? *"Behold, I go to prepare a place for you if it were not so..."* You'll be snubbing God by rejecting his priceless efforts and construction of a befitting Kingdom for you. No believer should miss that Kingdom as its worth is more than gold and treasures of great pearl. God is super interested in you. He is doing all He can to ensure that you don't miss it. See **(Revelations 3: 20)** *"Behold, I stand at the door, and knock: if any man hears my voice, and open the door, I will come into him, and will sup with him, and he with me."* The least you can do for yourself and the creator is to be ever ready.

2. The Devil is interested in your not being there. From the point of salvation, the devil drew a battle line over your life. He has not stopped roaming to and fro seeking whom he may devour. Knowledge of this should make you understand how precious Heaven is. How priceless the kingdom is, and how much serious you must be to get there. The devil doesn't waste his time and energy pursuing a course that isn't golden. His interest is genuinely born out of jealousy. Remember he as Lucifer was the most beautiful angel who lost his place. Since that fall, he vowed to fight against any member of

the human race that has decided to get access into the Kingdom. It's a fight for your life. It's a fight for your destiny. If you ignore, you'll all be gambling with your salvation.

> *It's a fight for your destiny.*

The Kingdom of God is not a place that any believer should miss. The sufferings, persecutions, temptations, and trials of our faith should prep us for the glorious Kingdom. We must look forward to the glorious appearance of our Lord and Saviour Jesus Christ, to usher us into the place that He has prepared for us. May we not miss the eternal blessing of His Kingdom in Jesus' name. Amen.

Chapter Reflections

- _____
  _____
  _____

- _____
  _____
  _____

- _____
  _____
  _____

MORE BOOKS BY KELAFO AND SHALLAYWA COLLIE

Go Global Leadership Keys: Strategies for Your Business, Brand and Organization to Have Global Impact

You are my Father; I am your Son - Understanding Kingdom Sonship (Revised)

A Lifetime Relationship: Life Building Time in the Presence of God, 52 Week Devotional for Men and Women

Victory: 21 Powerful, Prayerful Biblical Declarations to Begin Your Day

Heavenly Prayers to Live Inspired, Empowered and Fulfilled Daily (Revised)

Practical Keys to Knowing Christ to Walk In Deliverance, Purpose and Destiny (Revised)

For more materials, to connect with and book Dr. Kelafo and Shallaywa Collie, visit and subscribe to these platform:

www.kamgbahamas.com

www.kelafoczcollie.com

www.shallaywa.com

www.majesticpriesthoodpublications.com

YouTube: Kami Bahamas

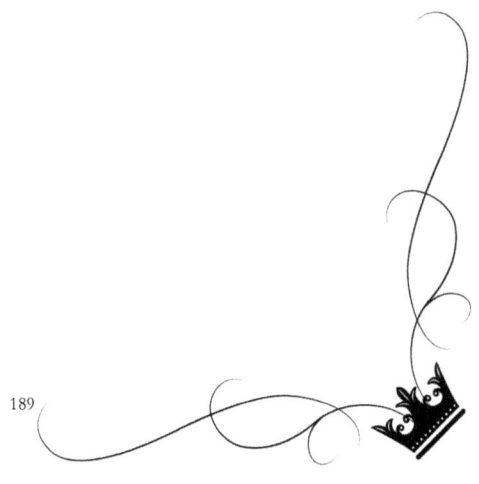

www.ingramcontent.com/pod-product-compliance
Lightning Source LLC
LaVergne TN
LVHW051557070426
835507LV00021B/2632